AGAINST ALL ODDS

THE MOST AMAZING TRUE-LIFE STORY YOU'LL EVER READ

PAUL CONNOLLY

JB

JOHN BLAKE

Published by
John Blake Publishing Limited,
3 Bramber Court, 2 Bramber Road,
London W14 9PB, England

www.johnblakebooks.com

www.facebook.com/johnblakebooks 🔲
twitter.com/jblakebooks 🔲

First published in paperback by Metro Publishing, an imprint of John Blake
Publishing, in 2010. Reformatted paperback edition published by John Blake
Publishing in 2017

ISBN: 978-1-78606-261-1

British Library Cataloguing-in-Publication Data:
A catalogue record for this book is available from the British Library.

Design by www.envydesign.co.uk

Printed in Great Britain by CPI Group (UK) Ltd

1 3 5 7 9 10 8 6 4 2

Papers used by John Blake Publishing are natural, recyclable products
made from wood grown in sustainable forests. The manufacturing processes
conform to the environmental regulations of the country of origin.

Every attempt has been made to contact the relevant copyright-holders,
but some were unobtainable. We would be grateful if the appropriate people
could contact us.

To my best friend in childhood, Liam Carroll.
Rest in peace, mate.

And to all the other boys and girls
from St Leonard's, many of whom are
also no longer with us.

Some names and locations have been
changed for legal reasons

CONTENTS

ACKNOWLEDGEMENTS

This book could not have been written without the seeds of self-esteem planted in me by Mary Cuckney, when I was still a child; special thanks to Mary.

Ian Mecklenburgh, Trevor Schofield and Chris Clapshaw have long been good friends and have always provided me with fantastic support. Thank you, guys.

I would also like to thank Deirdre Nuttall, who provided me with a writing service throughout the production of this book, from start to finish, and without whose assistance I would never even have had anything to send to the publisher.

Above and beyond all, thanks to Jo Cole, my partner in life and the mother of my two wonderful sons, Harley and Archie.

1

GROWING UP BAD

IT HAD BEEN many years since I had seen any of the children who had grown up with me, who had been my sisters and brothers throughout my childhood and adolescence. When I left the children's home at St Leonard's, I promised myself that I would have nothing to do with them ever again; that the past was over and the future, such as it was, was in my own hands. I was sure that my only chance of living a good life would be to put the past behind me, even though that meant saying goodbye to some of the people I loved the most – as well as the ones I hated more than words could even begin to express.

For people in my world, it was never good news when the police knocked on the door, and I had several good reasons to be anxious on this particular occasion. I knew them as soon as they turned up; police have a distinctive way of knocking that one becomes familiar with over the years. I peered out of the window at them to confirm my suspicions, but I didn't answer the door, hoping that they would just give up and go away quietly. I didn't think I had anything to answer for at present, in any case. I was used to avoiding contact with the police, usually with good reason.

They kept coming back, two female constables in plain clothes that did nothing to conceal the fact that they were police officers. Eventually, I decided that, if the police were really going to nick me, they would not have sent two women. The police knew me well and they knew that I would easily be able to take out two men, let alone a couple of girls, if I were so inclined.

I answered the door. I didn't open it all the way; I did not want to look too welcoming.

'What's up?'

The women looked at me with a degree of sympathy. One of them smiled. She was a real stunner; a gorgeous young woman whose formal, tailored clothing did nothing to hide her shapely body. I relaxed a little. I may have even smiled.

'Can we come in for a moment?'

'I suppose.'

I stood aside and the two women walked in the door of the first home I had ever owned and paid for on my own.

'You might want to sit down,' one of them

advised me. 'We've got bad news, and you should prepare yourself for a shock.'

'I'm fine.'

I stayed standing. I don't like people telling me what to do, especially in my own home, even if they are pretty young women.

'It's about St Leonard's.'

'St Leonard's? What about it?'

St Leonard's was the children's home where I had grown up, in the part of East London that spills over into Essex. I had not been inside its doors for years, and I did my best to think about it as little as possible. Years before, I had decided that I was fucked up enough on my own; I didn't need to have to deal with the stress of being around or even thinking about other fucked-up people. Quite the reverse – I needed to seek out the company of sane, normal people and focus as hard as I could on keeping things together for myself. That was the only way to sort my life out. I had cut all my ties with my past, my family and the children's home where I had spent the worst years of my life. If you lie in shit, you smell of shit.

I didn't want to smell of shit.

'What is it?' I asked the police officer. 'I haven't been to St Leonard's for donkey's years. What's all this got to do with me?'

'Paul, it has been brought to our attention that, of the eight children in your dorm, only two of you are still alive.' She paused. The two women looked at me solicitously.

I sat down. I was only thirty-five. Surely that wasn't right. How could all those boys with whom I had grown up be dead? It didn't make sense. I waited for her explanation. It turned out that six of us had died, several by slow suicide in the form of heroin abuse, and at least two by faster means.

'There have been complaints made of serious abuse, including sexual abuse, during the period when you were at St Leonard's. A major investigation is ongoing, and we would like to talk to you. We are going to have to talk to everyone who grew up in St Leonard's when you were there, but your name in particular has come up in some of the evidence we have been hearing. Apparently, you were a witness to the attempted rape of one of the other children...'

'Tell me what happened to the other boys,' I requested numbly.

The policewoman listed the names of the boys who had been like my brothers when I was growing up. One of my old friends, Mark Byrnes, had taken a dive into oblivion off Beachy Head. You've got to be more than a little desperate to do something like that. Liam, who had been my very best friend throughout all the years of my childhood, had jumped on the tracks at Mile End Station and died under the wheels of a commuter train. What could be worse than that? What had happened to him that had made him so desperate? I wasn't even sure that I wanted to know.

'He was schizophrenic, apparently,' the woman said of Liam's death, as if that was a mitigating factor. As if that made it less awful.

Liam was dead. Liam. I felt sick. I wanted to hold my head in my hands and close my eyes but I just sat and stared at her as she continued: 'We've started an investigation into the St Leonard's children's home, Operation Mapperton, to find out what went on there and why so few of you are still alive. We understand that you grew up in Wallis Cottage which was –' she checked her paperwork '– run by William Starling.'

Starling. I had not heard that name for years. In an instant, I was reduced to the little boy who had been told every day, 'You're rubbish. You'll never amount to anything. Look at you, you fucking retard. You Irish lowlife scum. You're just a bloody Connolly, aren't you? Prison fodder from the day you were born, you little shit. Who ever loved you? Nobody, that's who… and nobody ever fucking will.'

My parents were Irish, from the beautiful wilds of Connemara, on the windy Atlantic seaboard, on the most westerly coast of the European continental shelf. My father was the seventh son in a family of fourteen, and my mother, a trained midwife, was from a smaller family, also local. My father, Matthew, had grown up in a minuscule labourer's cottage in the middle of nowhere in rural Galway, and had a lot of poverty to escape from. My mother, Mary, was from rather more affluent circumstances; her father owned a local pub, which meant that he was one of the wealthier people in the area. I don't think he was very impressed when his daughter married a boy from a rough cottage. My parents had already had six children together when, like so many Irish people in the late fifties and early sixties, they came to look for work in the East End of London. Now, Connemara is one of Ireland's most loved tourist destinations, but back then it was a poor place, the rough stony ground challenging the local farmers to eke out a meagre living, and jobs and a good livelihood painfully difficult to come by.

The idea seems to have been that my father would make a living in the building trade in London, like so many Irishmen before him, and presumably my mother thought that she might pick up work as a midwife. In those days Irish health-care workers were very highly trained and, every year, thousands of London babies were delivered by Irish midwives. The money they sent back to Ireland when they emigrated helped to prop up the crippled economy of what was still a very backward island.

At that point, everything seems to have started

falling irreparably apart for my parents and for all their children. I don't know the details, but apparently my mother kicked my father out before I was even born, perhaps because she was seeing another man. I have never known either of my parents, but the impression I have gained was that my mum was an attractive woman with no shortage of attention from men.

When I was two weeks old, my mother left me out beside the rubbish bins near her home in Stepney Green. I was a small baby with jet-black hair. One of the neighbours heard my cries and took me in and called Social Services, who came and collected me and handed me into the care of the nuns of St Vincent's in Mill Hill, which was in Hendon in North London. I was the seventh son of a seventh son, but it did not bring me a lot of luck back then.

From the moment my mother dumped me on the side of the street with the rubbish, I would see her only a handful of times in the course of my childhood. I never knew her.

Together with scores of other babies, I would stay in St Vincent's nursery until I was four or five, and then move into a big dormitory with the other children. Although a great deal of this phase of my life is, of course, quite hazy, I have some memories from the period, and especially of our favourite game, which was to leave the dormitory by means of the window and then leap precariously from one window ledge to another, high above the ground. That must have been when I lost the first of my nine lives, because, if we had fallen, we would have been goners, that's for sure.

I also remember that, every so often, one of the children from St Vincent's nursery was adopted and taken away by new parents. For the rest of the children, this was amazing. One day our little friend would be there eating and getting dressed and undressed and going to bed with the rest of us, and the next he would be gone and we would be told that he had been taken away to live with a 'mum' and a 'dad'. The very concept of a nuclear family was not familiar to us, and the whole business seemed to be wrapped in a cloak of mystery.

As a healthy, white male who had been given up as a newborn, I should have been a prime candidate for would-be adoptive parents. In fact, one of the nurses at the home, Mary Littler, was very fond of me and tried to adopt me, even though she was still a very young woman at the time, about twenty years old. My mother put paid to that. Biological parents could veto any adoption of their children by displaying some meagre interest in their welfare, and I believe that my mother came to visit me about once a year, although I don't remember those visits and don't know why she was so resistant to having me adopted, as she clearly had no interest in me herself. Mary also told me that my father, who was then working nights, came to visit me every day when I was very small.

I have often wondered how my life would have turned out if I had become Mary's adopted son; if someone had loved me as a child, as I love my little boys today.

I am still in touch with Mary, who lives on the south coast now. She has provided me with some of the sparse information I have about my origins. Mary told me that my father had done his best to keep the family together after my parents separated, and that he had even got back with my mother at one stage so as to get all of us kids out of care, but that once again our mother had ensured that we would stay just where we were. After a while, my father drifted away, too. From that moment, both my parents became strangers to me and they have remained so ever since.

One of my earliest memories is that of reaching the age of three or four and suddenly realising in a moment of clarity that I was utterly alone in the world. Every child growing up in care has that realisation at an early age. All of a sudden, with awful, shocking clarity of vision, you know that you are all alone and that, ultimately, nobody even cares whether you live or die because the world is indifferent to the children who nobody loves. Nobody wants you. Nobody ever wanted you. It is the loneliest feeling in the world. It is utterly overwhelming. I have been through it myself and I have seen it happen, again and again, to the younger children in the home where I grew up. I think that, when this terrible realisation happened to me, I changed overnight from being quite a friendly, outgoing child to a difficult, shy child with a tendency to lash out that I have never managed to get completely under control. That dreadful understanding, of being utterly alone and unloved, shatters confidence and hope the way nothing else can.

Just before I turned eight, I was taken from the only home I had ever known and brought by my social worker Mr Gardner, an elegantly dressed black man, to St Leonard's Home for Children in Essex, on the outskirts of East London. The home was a complex of beautiful Victorian buildings that had been created in what was then the green Essex countryside, to provide London's unwanted offspring with a healthy country childhood that would give them a great foundation in life. By the time that I was sent to live there, in the late 1960s, London had grown so much that it had engulfed the countryside and the home, which was now run by Tower Hamlets. I had been told that I had a brother there, but we had not had any contact, so I did not know Declan any more than any of the other children I was about to meet. I knew that I had six brothers and one sister and I had met the ones closest to me in age, but I had little understanding of what being related meant. We had all been rejected by our mother, but the older ones had spent a large portion of their childhoods at home.

I am the youngest, after John. Then come Danny, Declan, Peter, Matthew, Michael and Anne. At least our mother had been consistent in not having any interest in any of her children. Several of my siblings had done time in St Vincent's, and Matty and Michael, who were much older, were in a more secure unit in Bedfordshire. We had nothing to do with each other then; we have almost nothing to do with each other now. I do talk to Matty once in a while on the phone, but we don't actually meet much. Blood is not really thicker than water; if you don't grow up with your sisters and brothers, they are not really family.

Back then, as I was brought to St Leonard's children's home, I wondered if Declan and I would get to know each other better. I was led by the hand down the long, winding avenue to the cottage I would share with about thirty other children and our house parent, Bill Starling, a man who was then in his mid-forties, having been at the home for about two years. I was told that we children were supposed to refer to him as 'Uncle Bill'. Some of the other care workers there were also referred to as 'Aunties' and there was one in particular who I had the misfortune of having as one of my carers. I can't tell you her real name for legal reasons but I'll refer to her simply as 'Auntie Coral'.

When I met up with Declan, he gave me some inside information. Until recently, the housemother who had been taking care of him had been a kind, older woman called Peggy, whom the children referred to affectionately as 'wooden tit' because of the prosthetic breast she wore following an operation for breast cancer. I do not know how Peggy felt about her nickname, but it did seem to be meant well. The children had all liked Peggy and she seemed to have provided them with a degree of security and some sense of being cared for. Unfortunately for me, Peggy had by now retired.

Starling was still quite new, and apparently Declan had not quite got the measure of him yet, or else did not want to talk about it for some reason. The Principal of the home was a man called Alan Prescott, and I was strongly advised by Declan and all the other kids I met to keep out of his way, for reasons that would soon become very clear.

At St Leonard's, there were fourteen 'cottages', each of which housed up to thirty kids. At the home, we had our own orchards, playground, sick bay, swimming pool and gardens. It all looked beautiful and someone had clearly put a lot of thought into building a wonderful environment for London's unwanted kids. We were there for all sorts of reasons, although I was in a minority, having been unceremoniously dumped by my mother as a babe-in-arms. We had rent boys who had been 'saved' from the streets as teenagers, riddled with sexually transmitted diseases and serious behaviour problems; children whose parents had voluntarily given them up for one reason or another; and children who had been taken from their parents by the social workers for the usual reasons of neglect, indifference and abuse. Occasionally, a child would come and stay at St Leonard's for a short period while his or her case was being decided, but the vast majority of us were there for the duration of our childhood and teenage years and, for us, St Leonard's was the only home that we knew.

We were all different, but we had one thing in common: we were all miserably, desperately unhappy. Not a lot of thought had gone into selecting the house parents who served at St Leonard's – or perhaps it had, albeit not in the way one would expect, and we certainly were not receiving anything even vaguely resembling proper childcare.

Before deciding to go into the care industry, Bill Starling had been a lorry driver. In those days, astonishing as it seems, there was no vetting system for house parents, and he had no particular experience in caring for children. For Uncle Bill, the job at St Leonard's was a way to skim the system, pocket the proceeds and brutalise the kids in the process. Most of us were very small and thin for our age, and the reason why was simple – we were fed on bread and margarine and not much else, while Starling used the housekeeping budget for himself.

On my very first night – remember that I was just eight years old and that I had just left the only home that I had never known – I wet the bed. Of course, I was desperately embarrassed. But, as if that was not bad enough, Auntie Coral made me strip off my sheets and then threw me and the sheets together into a bath of freezing cold water heavily laced with bleach where she scrubbed me until I was almost bleeding. This was the standard approach at St Leonard's to children with bedwetting problems. Unsurprisingly, Auntie Coral's attempts to cure us of bedwetting were less than effective. Most of the little ones wet their beds frequently, and the same treatment was always doled out.

I soon learned what happened when we children misbehaved in any way. Several times a week, we would be rooted out of our dorms and told to strip off all of our identical white-and-grey striped pyjamas – which resembled nothing more than the prison garb of caricature prisoners in old comic books – and line up in the hallway, while Starling, sometimes with some of his friends, walked up and down shouting, kicking our legs out from under us and stubbing out their cigarettes on our pigeon-chested bodies. They found this funny. They found it hilarious. Uncle Bill always had a cigarette in his hand. He was a chain smoker who lit up and puffed away in front of the children, regardless of what was going on. This also meant that he always had a handy tool at the ready to inflict pain on our tender skin.

When the adults had tired of the entertainment, we would be allowed to put on our nightclothes and leave. I do remember that this sort of thing would happen more often in the summertime. We would all be sent to bed at the usual early time but, because it was summer, it was still light, and none of us could sleep, so we would start messing about, tossing pillows and generally acting up. Then Bill Starling would come roaring up to the dormitory and root us out, yelling, 'Get out into the hall, you little bastards! Get the fuck out of bed, you little shits,' and the entertainment would begin, especially on those evenings when he had friends over and they had all been drinking. While Uncle Bill was not a particularly heavy drinker, a beer or two seemed to help him to shed whatever few inhibitions he still had. Uncle Bill liked to show his friends that the kids he was in charge of knew who the boss was, and he was single-minded in pursuit of this goal.

Apart from Uncle Bill's incursions into the dormitory, there was little at St Leonard's to break the monotony of everyday life. In the morning, we got up at around seven, got our breakfast and went to school. In the evening, we came home, ate, watched TV for a while and went to bed. We were periodically instructed to wash, and generally made to take care of ourselves in terms of personal hygiene. Nothing ever really changed, and every day was pretty much the same as the one that went before it in one long, depressing litany. Birthdays were not celebrated – which was at least honest, because we all knew that nobody was very happy about the fact that we unwanted rascals had been born. In fact, mine was usually marked in the form of birthday greetings on the second of August – when I had actually been born on the twenty-second. In a good year, a local factory would donate toys at Christmas, which we would all share, because there was little question of any child having personal possessions, which would have led inevitably to jealousy and squabbling. Christmas dinner stands out, as Christmas Day was the only day in the year when we would eat well. Some of the children would have gone home to see relatives for the holidays, so there would be less of us about, and we would have a proper roast turkey and other good things and stuff ourselves until we felt sick, and then watch the better-than-usual fare on television.

The kids of St Leonard's were a motley crew of mostly Irish and black boys and girls. They were the offspring of already dysfunctional families, like the Connollys, who had come to London with the idea that they would get ahead and prosper, only to find that the streets were not paved with gold after all. Their old problems were still with them and now there was no support system to hold everything together as there might have been at home. In those days, the perception was that the most dysfunctional people in Britain were usually either Irish or black, which is why, if you look at old news reels, you'll see the signs landlords used to post in their windows: 'No blacks, Irish or dogs'. Irish and black petty criminals flooded borstals and prisons, and most of the drunks cooling off in the police cells were from the same demographic. Even at the young age of the children in the home, we were seen as the lowest form of life there was, and treated accordingly.

It was not fair, but people who come from the toughest, hardest, most poverty-stricken backgrounds are often going to be the most difficult to deal with and the most likely to become dangerous, truculent people, and the most likely to get drunk and make a nuisance of themselves. I saw this for myself, growing up, and later when I visited a relative in borstal where he was serving time for mugging old ladies. In his lock-up, as elsewhere, the prisoners were mostly Irish or black – there were no white, English grammar-school boys there!

At the home, we children often got into fights, but we were also like sisters and brothers and, perhaps surprisingly, we were colour-blind. Nobody cared who was Irish and who was black because we had so much in common; we were all abandoned runts who had been thrown on the tender – or not so tender – mercy of the state. We would fight over the last scrap of bread on the table or what we watched on television, but we didn't care what colour anyone was or where their parents had come from.

My best friend at St Leonard's was a little boy called Liam Carroll – another Irish child – who was in much the same boat as me. Liam lived in the cottage directly opposite mine, Myrtle Cottage. The windows of our cottages faced each other and, when we had to return to our respective buildings, Liam and I would part reluctantly. We would go to our dormitories and wave at each other through the windows, a strangely comforting ritual. I can still remember seeing his pale face through the slightly warped old glass, as though I was looking at him underwater. I didn't know how Liam had ended up in the home. He had a bigger brother but I never learned how they had been abandoned and this was not something we ever discussed. I imagine that it was another sad little tale of dysfunction and lack of love.

Liam and I were inseparable for years. To this day, I have to say that he was one of the strongest people I have ever known. It seemed to me then that, no matter what life threw at him, Liam would be OK. Even as a child, Liam appeared to be a pillar of strength. The only really happy memories I have from my childhood involve Liam. We bunked off school together whenever possible, and made our way to a nearby field where horses bound for the abattoir were kept. We enlivened the final days of those unhappy horses by jumping on them and riding bareback until we fell off. When we did go to school, we would walk the five miles there so as to save our bus fare to spend on sweets and other cheap carbohydrates that made us feel briefly full.

On one occasion, all the kids from the home had been taken over to Holland to do a hundred-mile march from Nijmegen to Arnhem, together with a bunch of boy scouts in uniform. Finding ourselves in the local red-light district, Liam and I spent so long eyeballing the girls that we missed our lift back to the youth hostel in the depths of the forest, and had to make our own way back in the dark, getting there just before the search parties were sent out.

These might not sound like typically happy boyhood memories, but they are what I have and they make me smile. For me, Liam was a real big brother, and I think he loved me, too.

2

SCHOOL DAYS

I STARTED GOING to St Mary's Catholic School in Hornchurch when I was eight. Ostensibly, having been born to Catholic parents and baptised into the Church, I was being raised as a Catholic, and we all went through the motions of First Holy Confession, Holy Communion and Confirmation without understanding what it was all supposed to mean. The Church never intervened in any matters concerning our material welfare, and seemed to see us as nothing more than souls to claim for the Catholic God by dispensing the basic sacraments without explanation. The hypocrisy of the whole thing still makes me very angry. Presumably, my mother had eight children she clearly did not want because she was a Catholic and good Catholics do not use birth control. Heaven forbid! Having thus ensured our arrival into an unfriendly world, the Church did not seem to feel any further responsibility for us.

There was one positive figure in my life during this period, a fact for which I am hugely grateful. Mary, who had wanted to adopt me as a baby, had kept in touch with me, and was something of an aunt figure. By this stage, she had moved away from London and down to the New Forest on the south coast. Mary had married a kind man called Adrian and had a son of her own, Spencer, who was six years younger than me.

Bless her heart; Mary would invite me down every summer until I was about thirteen for a little holiday with her family at their home in Bournemouth. It was a different world. They had horses and stables and we would go to the beach every day in her little red Mini. Knowing that there was a real world in which people could be kind to each other was a lifeline to me; much more than I realised at the time. Mary was a kind, generous spirit who showed me how an adult woman could be nurturing and generous. As Adrian was usually working, I saw little of him, but he was a benign figure in the background. Their child, Spencer, was born when I was about six, and because of the age difference we didn't have that much to do with each other, although I remember him running about after me when he got a little older.

My short holidays with Mary and her family were extremely precious to me but, kind as she was, Mary's influence on me could not repair the damage that was being done in St Leonard's and at school. I was still illiterate at eleven when we took the 11-plus, which of course I failed. Attempting it had been bordering on the ridiculous and I don't know why the teachers even bothered to put my name down for it. From there, I went to the all-boys Bishop Ward Catholic School in Dagenham.

After the fiasco of the 11-plus, I largely gave up on school, skiving off whenever I got a chance. When I did turn up, I either got into a fight or got the cane. I was a poor kid from the children's home with a free dinner ticket, cheap clothes and a lot to prove. As I fell farther and farther behind the basic minimum standards I should have reached, my behaviour deteriorated until I posed a significant discipline problem in the classroom and was probably a danger to myself and others. School continued to be a complete nightmare as I grew older. The lessons were awful and we were locked in the rooms in an attempt to wield some control over us.

Because I had failed the 11-plus, I was put in the lowest class along with all the other dim kids. We were now the ones who had been labelled as failures. We accepted the general designation of ourselves as dunces, but even then I think that I knew on some level that I was brighter than most of the kids in the dunces' class. I was briefly put into a higher class, despite not being able to read and write, but I got upset because I wanted to be with my friends. All the Catholic kids from St Leonard's went to school together, and I didn't want to be away from my pals: my best friend Liam Carroll and two others. I felt that I needed to be with my friends because there was strength in numbers and I was glad when I was returned to the dunces' corner.

Skinny and undersized, ignorant and completely unaware of my potential, I was belligerent, bitter and angry way beyond my limited ability to verbalise those difficult feelings. Like the rest of the children in St Leonard's, I had very good reason to be angry. The cottage that I was supposed to call home was far from being a refuge, offering violence and beatings instead of home comforts.

On one occasion, my house father, Bill Starling, caught me bunking off school. Uncle Bill had been waiting behind the cottage door for me, and when I came back he grabbed me by the hair, punched and kicked me up two flights of stairs, saying, 'Get up there, you little bastard. Go on, you little fuck. I'll teach you to bunk off, I'll show you who the boss is around here...' Then Uncle Bill threw me off the balcony at the top. I landed heavily, breaking several ribs. I ended up in sick bay for a few weeks with my ribs bandaged tightly so that they could heal. I was philosophical about my stay in the sick bay; at least I didn't have to go to school.

So far as I know, there was no onus on Starling to explain or justify the injuries in any way. Certainly, it did not occur to me to make any sort of official complaint, because what had happened was not exactly an anomalous event in a home where violence was a daily occurrence. I don't even know if it would have been possible for me to complain, or to whom I could have gone. Perhaps files and reports were made about my unfortunate stint in sick bay, but as these would have been given to Principal Prescott, who was almost as dangerous as Starling, who was going to care?

You might be wondering how it was that nobody at school ever noticed that anything was wrong. For a start, most of the teachers either didn't look at or didn't care about the little scruffs from St Leonard's. They didn't like the blacks or Irish any more than the general population did. In fact, as they had to deal with us and our problems every day, they probably liked us even less. They saw their responsibility towards us as beginning and ending with keeping a certain amount of control in the classroom, and if that meant lashing out, so be it. As there was little expected of us in terms of academic achievement, there did not seem to be any feeling that we needed to be taught even basic literacy or numeracy skills. Sometimes another child's parent would say something like, 'Hasn't that little boy got an awful lot of bruises?' but an answer would always be supplied, along the lines of: 'Yes, he's a violent little boy. A bit of a problem, really. He had another one of his tantrums and he threw himself against the wall again.'

I did have one teacher who seemed worried about what was going on in St Leonard's. His name was Mr Molloy, another Irishman.

'What are you doing, Paul?' he would ask. 'Jaysus, why are ya always covered in cuts and bruises? You're a little ruffian. What have you been up to, at all?'

I would say, 'Yeah, sir, they beat me up in the home.'

'Would you go on outta that. They never did.'

In the 1960s and '70s, watching out for kids' general welfare was not seen as part of the teachers' remit.

To be fair to him, Mr Molloy did go down to St Leonard's and ask what was going on, only to be met with a blank wall.

'Paul Connolly?' they said. 'Let's have a look at his file.'

Starling had to write in my file every day – as he did in every child's – and I gave him plenty to write about so there would have been a weighty pile of papers on me.

'Last Thursday?' he or Auntie Coral, who he had no doubt instructed, would say. 'Let's see. Oh yes, Paul had another one of his violent tantrums. He was throwing himself against the wall again. He has an episode like that every other day. He's a troubled child. To tell you the truth, we are barely managing to contain him. No surprises where he is heading...'

Starling didn't have to answer to anybody; he was something along the lines of a dictator in his own little empire. He wrote the rulebook.

The year I turned eight, I was run over by a car when I was crossing the road to go to the shops. I know that if someone had explained to me how to cross a road I would not have been run over at all. The children from the home were all very accident-prone, simply because we were never taught simple, basic things such as the rules of the road. The car changed gears and I thought it was stopping to let me go but it ran me over instead. Nobody had ever told me about looking both ways before you cross the road, so I had not even acquired this very basic skill. The resulting injuries made me determined to get fit and strong, although I didn't know how. I just knew that I wanted to be able to stand up for myself because I saw with my own eyes, every day, what happened to the kids who went along with their victim status, and because I was afraid that my injuries would make me more vulnerable to attack from the people who were supposed to be taking care of us.

By this stage, I slept with a knife that I had stolen from the kitchen under my pillow – a long, sharp kitchen knife that would do some serious damage if called for. I didn't know how to use it properly – not yet – but knowing that it was there made me feel a little bit safer. When I was about to go to sleep, I would close my hand against the smooth wooden handle of the knife and it would give me more comfort than any teddy bear ever could.

The first time I met a real family was when a kid from my class in junior school invited me home to play one day after school. I was so overwhelmed by all the food on offer at my friend's house that I just put my head down and ate like a wild beast. I had never seen steak before. I ate until my stomach hurt, and then I looked around and took in those exotic creatures, mum and dad, and a house where the pictures were not nailed to the walls.

For the very first time, it began to dawn on me that the way we lived in St Leonard's might not be the norm; that there might be a different, better way to go about doing things. For the very first time in my short life, my yearning for something better began to take shape. I realised what I had been missing all this time – a family; a home.

By the time I was eight, I had already been identified in St Leonard's and at school as an extremely violent, difficult child, so it was not surprising that I was drawn to boxing. The original idea to get into boxing was Liam's. He was also a very small kid with a need to be able to stand up for himself, and I imagine that his motivations must have been very similar to mine. We used to walk to school together, and the route took us past Dagenham Boxing Club. Liam and I used to wonder what went on in there and we often speculated about it.

One day, Liam said, 'Come on, Paul. Let's go in. Let's see what they are doing in there.'

'Do you think they'll have a pop at us?' I asked. I liked his idea, but I was also a little intimidated at the thought of just going into the club.

'Dunno. They might, I s'pose.'

'I suppose we can always leg it if they do.'

'Yeah.'

'Come on, then.'

We went in nervously and poked our heads around the door. There were some men inside. They were clad in sportswear, and chatting to each other amiably as they worked out. We were sure they were going to shout at us and tell us to fuck off because we were just kids from St Leonard's and everybody hated us. Instead, two friendly men looked at us with smiles.

'Come on in, lads,' they said. 'We won't bite your heads off.'

Liam and I looked at each other. Did they really mean it? We shrugged. There was nothing to lose.

We went in gingerly, but they really were friendly; they were not just pretending. Even when they saw our cheap uniforms and bad haircuts, they were not put off. This was the first time that anything of the sort had ever happened. Even when we told them where we were from, they did not recoil from us. What was going on?

'Do you want to put some gloves on, lads?' they asked. 'Do you want to have a little move around?'

I looked at Liam. Liam looked at me.

'All right, then.'

It was just a rundown gym in the local boxing club, but venturing into the Dagenham Boxing Club was absolutely the best thing that had ever happened to me. Liam and I were boxers after that, two wiry little runts together, beating out our aggression with our small, bony fists. Because Liam and I were both so small and underweight for our ages, people assumed that we were much younger than we actually were. They could not believe it when we told them our real ages.

Although the facilities were very basic, and I was just put in front of a bag with gloves on and told to hit it, getting involved in boxing was a revelation to me, and a real milestone in my young life. For a start, I had my first experience of being with adult men who were not only not violent and dangerous, but also were actually friendly and kind. And they were not just pretending to be kind; they really meant it. The boxing coaches were good with children, and they gave Liam and me the closest thing to proper childcare that we had ever received. The teachers at school caned us and battered us. The care workers in the home beat us up. So far as the social workers were concerned, we were just a series of boxes to be ticked. Our parents had been missing in action for as long as we could remember. These guys actually taught us useful stuff, gave us sandwiches and even listened to us with every appearance of interest. It was amazing. It was wonderful.

For a long time, I didn't go to the boxing club to learn about boxing, but just to have the experience of someone being nice to me. I am sure that to them it was no big deal, but for me it was huge.

Uncle Bill and Auntie Coral and Liam's house parents were not impressed with our new involvement with boxing, and they tried to stop us from going to the club. But Liam and I were not stupid. Now that we had adults on the outside who actually cared about us, even just a little bit, the abuse we were getting at home receded somewhat. Any child who had an adult in his life who might conceivably ask, 'Why is he getting bruised and hurt all the time?' was less likely to be badly damaged. I suspect that the families involved with the boxing club had an idea that things were bad in St Leonard's, because they would come to the home and collect us when we had to attend boxing events. They would have asked questions if we hadn't turned up when we should. This was the first time anyone but Mary had shown any interest in me at all and it was fantastic. While I can hardly say that my self-esteem flourished, some delicate green shoots did begin to appear.

Liam was quite good at boxing, but I was better. I started to realise that I had potential when I did my first gym show, which is a very carefully controlled fight and is all that young kids are allowed to do. The boys fight, but the whole thing is stopped the minute someone gets hurt. I won my first gym show when I was ten years old. After that, I could not be stopped. I won one thing after another until winning became the norm for me. It no longer mattered whether or not I could read and write and do sums, because now I had a plan; I was going to be a professional boxer. This also meant that I had to spend a huge amount of time at the gym, which was fine for me. The less time I spent at St Leonard's, the better.

I remember the trainers well: Lenny Wilson, Alan Mayhew and Tommy Butler. They and their wives would have Liam and me round to their homes and feed us what seemed to us to be glorious meals, although no doubt it was the sort of ordinary fare that they had every day. Some of the other kids' mothers would bring food to the club – just ordinary ham sandwiches and things like that, but it was so delicious compared to what we got in St Leonard's, it was wonderful.

Between the boxing and the improvements to my diet, I started to get healthier and stronger, although I would never be very big. Starling continued to try to discourage my boxing, but, now that I had friends, he could not stop me from going. He and Auntie Coral increasingly left me to my own devices, which suited me very well. I felt better able to control my sphere, and the less I had to do with them, the better. Even when Uncle Bill put me through a glass window once for reasons that I no longer remember, cutting my head badly, I was just sent to hospital on the bus with a towel wrapped around my head and blood trickling down the back of my neck, with no adult to make sure I got there and back in one piece. At the time, this did not seem even remotely odd. The social worker was told that I had slipped in the bath and fallen through the window. I didn't challenge the lie. What was the point?

While boxing certainly did not make me any less violent, it enabled me to focus and channel my anger and to control my aggression and temper so that I could use them for my own purposes, rather than just lashing out indiscriminately. Because I had always been undersized and underweight, from a very early age I wanted to be able to take care of myself. Boxing was the ideal way and fortunately I was very good at it. It showed me how important it was for things to be organised and orderly and disciplined, which was a lesson that I absorbed very well – and perhaps even a little too well. Although it might sound strange, it was also through boxing that I learned about love and respect and how family members can care for each other. As well as the coaches, some of the families of the other boys in the club took pity on me and had me round for meals, to feed me up. Of course, I always ate ravenously. I also seized the chance to look at ordinary family homes and all the usual accoutrements: family photos, fridges full of food, mums and dads who smiled and said encouraging things and didn't just curse and swear and swat their kids around the head. Knowing that there was another world out there stood me in good stead later in life, when I was in a position to make choices that would impact seriously on my future.

Most of the children at St Leonard's were much less fortunate.

Because I had been abandoned as a newborn, I had never known my mother, who was now living in Clapton in East London, but some of my older siblings had a degree of contact with her and, when I was about twelve, Danny and John suggested that I should go and visit. The older ones used to go up every few months and get a bit of guilt money from Mum and they recommended this as a thing that I would like to do, as all the kids appreciated having a little money to spend on sweets, especially because we were all on slim pickings at the home and were constantly hungry. All I had to do was show up and listen to her standard rant about how nothing that had happened was her fault in any way. It was a short ride on the train to Bethnal Green and on the bus through Hackney to Clapton, and I went on my own.

That was how I saw my mother for the last time in my life, and the first time that I can remember. She was living on her own at that time, and the idea was that I would spend the whole day there so as to get to know her a little. She told me to go to the shop across the road to get her something. On my way, I turned and shouted, 'Mum, what was it you wanted?'

She came out and went crazy, hissing, 'Don't you call me Mum around here!' She did not want anyone to know that she had children. Why, I do not know. Perhaps she didn't want her neighbours to know that she had abandoned all eight of her kids. I felt as though I had been slapped in the face.

Among the men whom my mother was seeing was an Irish builder, a big beefy man with huge arms, who was there when I called around. When they didn't want me to know what they were talking about, they spoke to each other in Irish.

Feeling ignored, I decided that I did not have a mother. After all, I had my boxing.

I think that I saw my father once or twice during my childhood; although I don't remember him very well. Seeing him was like visiting someone I didn't know. By this time, he was living in Hackney with a woman called Betty, and to me he just looked like any older man I might have passed in the street without giving him a second glance. I felt quite indifferent towards him. I don't know how he felt about me, but I do know that I was never visited by either of my parents during my time at St Leonard's.

Many children who grow up in care have daydreams about how, one day, they will return home, and life will be lovely and Mum and Dad will explain how it was all one big, horrid mistake that should never have happened. As for me, I never really entertained any dreams of getting back with my parents, and visiting them didn't make any difference. At least I had my boxing. At least I could take care of myself. Or so I thought.

But all my bravado did not stop me from getting hurt by my caregivers or out in the world. When I was thirteen, I got knocked over by a bus on a zebra crossing in East London, breaking my arm.

'You stupid little fuck,' was Auntie Coral's comment. 'You had it coming.'

But remarks like that didn't seem to matter as much as they used to.

I was beginning to understand that life at St Leonard's was even worse for many of the other kids.

3

ALL IN THE FAMILY

I think, looking back, that the saddest thing about the abuse – sexual and otherwise – at St Leonard's was that most of the kids in the home didn't even realise that it was strange or unusual for our carers to find sexual pleasure in the children's prepubescent bodies, or for teenage boys and girls to have to sleep with male and female house parents whenever they clicked their fingers in exchange for what should have been basic rights, such as decent food to eat and reasonably good quality clothes to wear. Although it may seem strange to anyone who grew up in a normal family environment, so far as we were concerned, this was just the way adults behaved because, quite simply, this was the way that the majority of the adults in our lives did behave. It was all most of us knew and we didn't even question it. We honestly believed that this was just the way the world worked. For many of us, the first inkling that our childhoods had not been normal didn't come until we left the home and moved away.

Looking back, I have realised that the situation at St Leonard's with respect to the sexual abuse must have been far more organised than it seemed to me at the time, and I wonder how extensive the organisation was, although I suppose that I will never know the whole story.

Just as girlie girls are attracted to hairdressing and tough guys to door work, paedophiles are attracted to working with children. Well, obviously. One of the questions potential care workers are asked at interviews is: 'Do you like children?' Then, once there are enough of them in the system, I guess it is easy for the whole thing to be perpetuated. Perhaps there is a secret handshake of some kind. I do know that institutionalised sexual abuse was far more common than anyone would like to think. I hope that this is still not the case, and the social workers I have met in recent years have assured me that the situation for children's care today is very much better than it was for my generation. But it is hard to be overly optimistic.

At St Leonard's, all the house parents and other care workers socialised with each other and seemed to have few friends on the outside, and I assume that everyone who lived and worked in the home knew what was going on with respect to sexual contact between the caregivers and the children, even if not everyone was actively involved with it to the same extent. I suppose that, just as the situation seemed 'normal' to us kids, so it must have to those caregivers who had lost all touch with reality and the way the outside world functioned. They all collaborated at work, and then after work they would pop over to each other's cottages for a drink and a few cigarettes. They lived on site with apartments in the same buildings as the children's rooms and they had absolute control over their small kingdoms and all their small subjects.

The Principal, Alan Prescott, was not just a notorious pederast whom all the children feared with very good reason, but also a local magistrate and a prominent local character, so the caregivers didn't have to worry about any repercussions from him; he was in it up to his neck. There was literally nobody to whom the care workers had to answer. The Tower Hamlets authorities were about fifteen miles away. I don't know how closely they supervised St Leonard's but there certainly was no sign of any interference from them. There were domestic staff who would come in to clean and I don't know if they were involved in the rampant abuse of the kids, but I think not. For one thing, they had much less contact with the children and, for another, I noticed that in the cottage in which I lived our 'carers' tended to lay off their most unwelcome attention when they were around, and to greet the cleaners with cheery smiles and hellos as if they were the most normal people in the world.

'How are you?' Uncle Bill would enquire cheerfully, as if he had not been meddling with a pair of under-sixes just half an hour earlier. 'Back to clean up after the wretches!'

I am not sure exactly when I realised what was going on, but it must have been when I was about nine or ten. As I had been eight when I was sent to St Leonard's, I was already too old to attract the interest of Bill Starling, who had taken a dislike to me from early on, in any case. Some of the children had been with Starling from a very early age – as young as four or five – and had been groomed by him to take part in sexual activities with Uncle Bill from when they were little more than preschoolers.

I think that the saddest aspect of this was that these kids had no idea that their lives were anything other than ordinary. Five was a good age to start sexual contact with Uncle Bill, so far as he was concerned. Children who caught his attention were selected by him for special treats, and brought into his private living room. They would emerge later, having been fed biscuits and sweets and given toys. They paid dearly for those presents, but at the time the rest of us just envied them, because we thought that that meant that somebody loved them, at least a little bit.

I particularly remember a couple of the girls. They were pretty little things, Irish like me. In our cottage, we all resented them bitterly because they seemed to be Starling's little pets. The rest of us kids were very jealous when they got taken away and given treats and no doubt there was a certain amount of bullying of the children who seemed to be the house parents' favourites. They were about five and six at the time, and both Starling and Auntie Coral were very affectionate towards them indeed. Now, I can only shudder at the thought of what those little girls probably had to do to earn those treats.

It is very difficult to explain to anyone who has not been there how strangely normal it can feel to know that the adults in your life are interested in your body in a way they shouldn't be. That was the culture in St Leonard's, and we were all utterly accustomed to it to the extent that it modified our behaviour on a daily basis.

Standards of personal hygiene were quite high at St Leonard's and we were all exhorted to bathe regularly. Even the children who had not been singled out for direct sexual abuse knew that bath time was a difficult time, when Uncle Bill and sometimes Auntie Coral would find a reason – any reason, no matter how spurious – to come in to the bathroom to see you in the nip and make a ribald comment or two. We learned that the best time to bathe was when the domestic staff were there at work, because then Starling was much less likely to find a reason to barge in on a bathing child. Bathing in the evening or at night was commonly known to be a risky activity, and most of us avoided it at all costs.

Many of the staff at St Leonard's were also having sexual relationships with the older kids, and here the dynamic could be different and much more ambiguous than the straightforward abuse of the little ones. While these relationships were clearly hugely inappropriate, not just because of the great difference in age but because of the power dynamic at play – we are talking about young people having sexual relations with the adults who were supposed to be providing them with mother and father figures – they were not simply examples of rape and abuse. Many of the teenagers were willingly engaging in sexual encounters because, for them, this behaviour had become a normal way of earning brownie points from the adults in their lives. In many cases, they had been accustomed to having to have sex with adults since before they had even come to the home.

St Leonard's was home to quite a number of young lads who had been 'saved' by the social workers or police from working as rent boys on the streets. These were kids who came from backgrounds as bad as any you could imagine. Just think of children being so desperate – aged just twelve or so – that they will take to the streets to sell their small bodies to whoever shows interest, risking the sexually transmitted diseases and the beatings that come as part and parcel of that way of life. These boys had been 'saved' by the police and social workers only to be sent to St Leonard's where their bodies were once again fair game for the adults. But now they were not even getting any money in exchange for their favours, and they did not have the option of running away because, if they did, they would just be sent straight back again. Talk about out of the frying pan and into the fire.

There were also teenage boys who were summoned to have sex with some of the female care workers, and who did not even mind, because who doesn't like sex? It was screwed up, but in a strange way, in the cottage where I grew up, having scored with Auntie Coral was a bit of a rite of passage for a lot of the boys. Despite her mean disposition, Auntie Coral wasn't bad looking. She was quite attractive and was probably not getting her leg over at home, so she made up for it with the boys she was supposed to be taking care of. My older brother Peter, who had been at St Leonard's before I appeared on the scene, had had sex with

Coral loads of times; he recommended it, just as a bit of light relief. Peter was a good-looking kid, and she liked them handsome. I am very happy to say that Coral never gave me the glad eye. She hated me way too much.

There was another woman who also worked at the cottage, and she liked young boys even more than Auntie Coral did. She was out of control. I remember her coming into the boys' dorm early in the morning to see for herself, in her own words, 'who had the biggest willy'.

'Out of bed, lads,' this woman would shout. 'I want to see a bit of skin. Ooh, go on, don't be shy. Let me see your willies. I won't hurt you.'

At some point during my ten years at the home, it was rumoured that Coral had a baby, and we all assumed that it had been fathered by one of the boys who she was supposed to be taking care of. Nobody had any proof, but that was what everyone was saying.

It was not until later that we would think about how inappropriate it had been for a woman who was supposed to be in the role of their mother to get her leg over with her male charges. Sex was everywhere at St Leonard's and at the time we did not discuss it much. We didn't have to; it was just a normal part of life, like having bread and margarine for lunch and dinner.

One particular boy came to live at St Leonard's

when he was about thirteen. I'll call him Simon (not his real name). Shortly after his arrival, we all knew that he was one male member of staff's special friend and that, for some reason, Simon was treated very differently from the rest of us. In fact, Simon slept regularly in this staff member's flat and, in return for whatever went on there, he ate well and was generally taken care of in every material way. Simon had better meals and nicer clothes than the rest of us, and we all assumed – not unreasonably – that this was because of whatever it was he was asked to do by his older friend, although, of course, I don't know the specific details of the nature of their relationship. The special attention would continue until Simon died of a heroin overdose, years later.

I have since wondered how so much sexual abuse could go on without anyone finding out about it and shutting the place down. Unfortunately, we now know that St Leonard's was far from unique, begging the question as to how high the abuse went and to what extent the abuse of England's rejects wasn't just accepted but perhaps even expected and seen as appropriate in certain circles. Prescott, the Principal of St Leonard's, was a magistrate, for crying out loud, and a very senior social worker in the area. He was a very prominent local citizen who was well known and respected everywhere he went. Did everyone know about what was happening at St Leonard's and choose to turn a blind eye? Did the authorities somehow think that it was all OK or that, as the rejects of society that they were, the foundlings of St Leonard's somehow deserved all they got?

But, realistically, who was going to care about what was happening to a bunch of black and Irish louts? The teachers in school just saw us as problems to be kept quiet. I don't know if they were aware of the sexual abuse that was going on in the home. Plenty of people would cross the street to avoid us and, to be fair, we gave them a lot of good reasons to do so.

We each had an assigned social worker who came every six months, and a fat lot of use they were. My social worker would sit down with me in the dining room twice a year, with Starling or Auntie Coral there too, just to make sure that everything was all right.

'How are things going then, Paul?' she would ask. 'Everything OK with you?' She would sit there with her pen poised to take a note and usually she would not even bother looking me in the face. I always suspected that she hated me, or was scared of me. Why else did she not want to look at me?

I would look at Auntie Coral. She would look back at me. She didn't say anything. She didn't have to.

'Yeah, OK,' I would say. 'Things are OK.'

Then the social worker would look at the file about me, where Starling had written down all the latest complaints about my behaviour and the many problems that they had keeping me in line. Perhaps understandably, she was taken in by what had been written in my file. I was invariably described as a very violent child – which I was – but how would this woman know the underlying reasons for my rage when it was presented by Starling as me who was the problem? And thank God I was violent, because that is one of the reasons, if not the reason, why I escaped from the horrendous sexual abuse that was the fate of so many of the other children. I had just one very narrow escape. Alan Prescott, the Principal, came in to my cottage one day when I was about thirteen and just beginning to go through the changes of puberty. I was ironing some clothes in the day room, and he staggered over to me drunkenly and leaned against me.

'Hello, Paul, lad,' he said. 'How are you today?' He tried to give me a winning smile. I could feel his stubby erection, hard against my leg, and see the burst veins and the enlarged pores on his face. There was a pimple on his upper lip. His large paunch pushed against my skinny ribcage. I could smell the booze on his breath and the rank stench from his armpits. I was suspicious of him and I wasn't going to take any chances. He was lucky he didn't get an iron in the face. Instead, I drew out my knife – I always carried a knife down the back of my trousers – and went ballistic.

'Don't fucking touch me, you fat cunt!' I shouted. 'I'll cut your fucking balls off. Get the fuck off me, you fat cunt!'

Prescott started drunkenly backing away towards the neighbouring television room, gathering speed as he went. His belly wobbled with the effort.

'Don't mess with me, Connolly,' he said rather weakly. 'Or I'll make you regret it.'

But I could see the fear in his eyes and it gave me courage.

Prescott slammed the day-room door behind him and held it closed with all his strength as I pressed against it, trying to get at him with the knife. I slammed my knife into the wooden door, over and over again.

Prescott continued to lean all of his considerable weight against the door. 'Come and help me, you little idiots!' he shouted.

The children who had been watching television ran over to help him hold the door closed. They were terrified. Nobody wanted me to get into the room with my knife. I stabbed the door over and over again until I was exhausted and it was full of holes. Finally, after what seemed like hours, I stopped. My breath was ragged. A tense silence was perceptible as, slowly, Prescott and the children on the other side of the door began to walk away.

I wanted to cry, but I didn't. I just left and went outside to the gardens to be on my own.

That was the first time that any of the staff had ever tried it on with me and I intended for it to be the last. Fortunately, after that, they all seemed to decide that I was just more trouble than I was worth. They tended to go for the softer touch; for gentler children who didn't have the means or ability to stand up for themselves.

Because I was never abused myself, I can't tell you about the details of what went on. Those stories can only be told by the victims, or by those of them who have survived. There was just one case that I was a direct witness to, when Bill Starling tried to rape a young girl who was about thirteen at the time. She was a gorgeous girl with blonde hair and a developing body that had caught the eye of the boys of around her own age – and of Bill Starling, although she was quite a bit older than the girls who usually interested him. I suppose that she was just so pretty that Uncle Bill decided to make an exception. I was walking past the girls' dorm one night when I heard a lot of noise – thumps and screams. I stuck my head around the door.

'What's going on?' I asked.

Uncle Bill, who was then in his fifties, was on top of this girl, trying to rape her. I could see her wide, terrified eyes and Uncle Bill's fat, hairy hand across her mouth.

'Fuck off, you,' he said, looking at me over his

shoulder. 'Get out of here. This is none of your business. This is between her and me.'

'I ain't going nowhere,' I told him. 'I'm staying right here until you leave her alone.' I stayed.

Years later, when this victim gave her testimony to the police, she told them that she would have been raped for sure, if I had not stayed. I was just in the right place at the right time – for her that is. Frustrated by being thwarted, Uncle Bill laid into me instead. He beat me up, and then he pushed one of the small wardrobes in the girls' dorm on top of me. Considering the way we lived in St Leonard's, this was water off a duck's back so far as I was concerned. I was happy that I had got one over on Uncle Bill and that I had been able to stop the girl from being raped.

Another of the care workers spent a great deal of time with one of his young charges throughout her time at the home. When she was between sixteen and eighteen, just out of the home, and he must have been in his fifties, they got married and he moved her into his house. You would think that such an unlikely and inappropriate marriage would have caused alarm bells to ring with the social workers – surely that isn't right? This girl went straight from a children's home into married life with one of her former caregivers, while she was still an adolescent. Even if, as may have been the case, there had been no sexual activity between them when she was still a minor, she might as well have been marrying her own father. Who was watching these people? How can this marriage have been allowed to take place, apparently unquestioned?

I already told you how boxing saved me from myself. It turns out it probably saved me from the sexual abuse, too. There was a huge difference between the treatment received by the kids who had people who cared about them on the outside and the ones who did not. There were some kids who even had parents whom they visited occasionally and others who had aunties and uncles or grandparents who took an interest. Some would go home for the weekend and get taken out once in a while to do things. These children were not abused, or at least were not abused as badly, because Starling and his friends knew that there was someone who cared about them in the outside world. They were even fed better, because the house parents knew that, if they were really badly treated, someone would notice and there might be some payback. I remember a couple of Jewish kids who had parents living locally who retained contact with them and possibly saw them at the weekends. Because there was someone looking out for them, they were given proper meals and spared the beatings that were daily fare for the rest of us. We would all sit down for meals, and they would have a different meal set in front of them to the rest of us.

I didn't have parents who cared about me, or aunties and uncles to visit on the outside, but, thanks to my involvement at Dagenham Boxing Club, I did have boxing coaches who took a paternal interest in me, and their wives, who did more for me than anyone in my own family ever had.

When we kids started getting into our teens, fumbling around with the opposite sex was on the cards and most of us did not hold back whenever the opportunity for some sexual activity presented itself, as it did pretty often. For one thing, when you get a mixed bunch of teenagers together – any teenagers, even the well-brought-up ones from good families – the hormones are going to fly, bras are going to be opened and a lot of teenage sperm is going to be spilled. For another, many of the inmates of St Leonard's were already very sexually experienced by the time they hit puberty, and they were more than ready to start initiating sexual experiences themselves, if only so that they could feel in control of a situation in which they had always been victims before. All children learn by imitating the behaviour of the adults in their lives, and the children at St Leonard's were no different.

There were more boys than girls at the home, so sexually available girls were very much in demand. After bedtime, us boys would get up and sneak over to the girls' rooms to see if we could get a little action. I remember some of the girls very well.

There was a beautiful girl of about fifteen who I'll call Angela (not her real name) who was very popular because she was so damn good-looking and sweet along with it. The same lad who was rumoured among the kids to have supposedly got Auntie Coral knocked up was also doing her. As a result of her interest in this lad, Auntie Coral hated Angela, whom she saw as a rival, and had it in for her, especially when he and Angela became a serious item. Auntie Coral did her best to make poor Angela's life an absolute misery and it says a lot for how Angela felt about this boy that their teenage relationship lasted as long as it did.

One of the first girls I ever really fancied, when I was about thirteen, was a gorgeous mixed-race girl with long, loose curls that tumbled down her back. Again, to protect her identity, I can't tell you her real name but I'll call her Maria. She was a real stunner with beautiful copper-coloured skin and eyes you could have drowned in. Maria even showed a little interest in me. Well, I was hooked and fancied myself in love.

One of my friends and I sneaked over to the girls' dorms one night and found Maria in a little nightie with her glorious brown legs bare and her slim body on display. She was kind enough to let me get close so as to steal a kiss, but I didn't get very far with her. I had no idea what I was doing. I had just managed to lean against Maria's warm, nightie-clad body when I suddenly ejaculated inside my pyjamas. Shit.

'I've got to go,' I stammered. 'Sorry ... just ... I've got to go.'

Horribly embarrassed, I ran back to the boys' bedroom and could not bring myself to speak to Maria for over a week. I was sure that all the girls must have been laughing about me among themselves. The friend who I'd sneaked over with, who was bolder, more confident and vastly more experienced, stayed behind, getting some action in bed with one of the other girls.

Some of the girls in St Leonard's ended up getting pregnant when they were still far too young to be mothers, and it is very surprising that more of them did not. There was one girl who used to do line-ups with all the boys, letting us take turns to have our way with her. I remember her wearing a pair of nylon knickers with a big love heart on the crotch. At one point, the carers thought that the poor girl might be pregnant and made her do a test. All the boys got into terrible trouble for what they had done, although, to be honest, I don't think there was ever the remotest chance of her really getting knocked up. I was one of the boys who climbed on top of her in a ditch in the local park, and all that ever happened was that the boy whose turn it was got excited straight away and ejaculated stickily on her skinny, white thigh. I don't think anyone ever actually got inside. We were all just between ten and thirteen at the time. Poor girl. We boys thought it was great that she was prepared to go so far for a bit of a laugh; she was probably just looking for affection in the only way she knew how.

Being children and teenagers, we obviously wanted to have fun when we could and one of the things we all enjoyed was singing. For some reason, all the boys in our dormitory were convinced that they could sing, including me. Back then it was all Motown, James Brown and Wilson Pickett – afros and high-waist trousers and cheap cologne – and so that's what we sang, kicking up a racket to see who was the best singer of them all. I'm telling you, we had some fun! What added to the excitement was that we never knew how Uncle Bill would react when he caught us out of bed and singing when we were supposed to be going to sleep. If he was in a good mood, he would just stick his head in the door and tell us to shut the fuck up or make us take off all our clothes and stand in the hall for a while – but if he was in a bad mood, well, anything could happen, and often did. It was kind of like playing Russian Roulette; that was the beauty of it.

When my room mates got tired of singing, I had more ideas about how we could entertain ourselves. I would insist that everyone got out of bed, and made them go through the work-out routines that I had learned at the boxing club. I put them through their paces, telling them that it would be to their benefit to know how to take care of themselves, and that being fit and strong would really help them to achieve this. I very much enjoyed being the instructor and passing on what I had learned.

Everyone knew that St Leonard's was haunted and we had all heard the stories of the three nuns who were supposed to wander up and down the corridors. Many of us also believed that we had had encounters with the ghosts. Most of us had experienced the feeling of an unseen person sinking down on to our bed when we lay down to go to sleep. One night I turned off the light and got into bed, only to feel a cold hand pressing down on my chest. I jumped back up and turned on the light, but there was no one there. Despite the fact that we were all sure that there were ghosts on the premises, none of us found the thought even remotely frightening. It was just something that we accepted to be true, and we all knew that we had much more to fear from the living than from any spectral vision. The care workers, too, just accepted that we shared our living quarters with the undead. We were all extremely matter-of-fact about it; it was what it was.

On some nights, after the small children had gone to bed and long after they were supposed to be asleep, I would hear one of them crying and go to see what was going on and if there was anything that I could do to help them in their distress. A lot of us bigger kids took an interest in the little ones and tried to be kind to them as best we could because we could remember all too well what it had been like to be in their situation a few years earlier.

What was invariably happening was that those tiny children had just realised that they were all alone in the world. That nobody wanted them. That nobody had ever wanted them. That nobody cared. That, ultimately, nobody really gave a shit whether they lived or died because they were essentially disposable. Disposable little scraps of humanity about whom nobody had ever cared. I remembered going through that myself. I think we all did. It is the loneliest feeling in the world. It is a feeling of utter, absolute desolation. It was almost worse watching someone else experiencing that realisation than it had been experiencing it for myself.

We older kids would talk to the little ones and try to help them work through what they were experiencing. We would say, 'Well, yes, you are all alone in the world, but there's nothing you can do about that. We're all alone too, and look at us, mate; we're all right.' What else could we say?

But they would not stop crying and asking, 'Why haven't I got a mummy? Why haven't I got a daddy?'

'It's all right,' we would say again. 'It's all going to be OK. It's not your fault.' We couldn't answer their questions, because we didn't have any answers and because many of us had not stopped asking the same questions about ourselves, even if we no longer allowed ourselves to break down.

The fact was that it did not make a blind bit of difference whose fault it was. For most of those kids, the damage had already been done.

And the only people they could conceivably turn to either beat them up or sexually abused them or both.

I told myself that I could not wait to leave.

4
ROUGH BOY

By the time I hit my teens, I was two people. On the one hand, boxing taught me to respect myself. I knew that I was very good at what I did, and I knew that the main reason for this was the fact that I worked tirelessly to reach my goal, putting in long hours in the gym and listening carefully to and acting on everything my trainers told me. But there was another side to my personality that was very unpleasant indeed. I was a thug, and knowing how to box meant that, when I was violent, I really knew what I was doing. I knew how to hurt people so badly that they would be walking around with the scars for the rest of their lives after an encounter with me.

While I would have knocked the lights out of anyone who had dared to suggest to me that I didn't like myself, around this time I more or less consciously decided to lose contact with Mary and her family. Despite the fact that she had always been so kind to me – or maybe even because she had always been so kind to me – it no longer seemed appropriate for me to be having cosy little holidays with Mary and her family in the New Forest. They represented all that was middle class and clean and decent, and I already knew that I was going down a route that Mary would have seen as the wrong path. I hardly even felt as though I belonged to the same species as her. The boxing club had become my point of contact with the real world, and I lost interest in staying in touch for a while. Looking back now, however, I can see that Mary was a real touchstone for me all through the years of my early childhood and I was never as grateful then as I should have been. Now, I realise that I can't thank Mary enough for everything she did for me.

Over the years, I would use my carefully honed boxing skills in a very wide range of circumstances and environments, from the boxing arena to the street. As an adolescent, I started to win amateur titles, even though I was so small I rarely weighed enough to box with opponents my own age. The fact that I was little and skinny could be to my advantage, because my opponents tended to underestimate me, at least for the first few moments of any encounter. I looked as though a strong gust of wind might blow me away, but I was able to punch well above my weight. I gained a degree of confidence from doing well in the boxing ring and learned to judge my own value according to how well I was doing at boxing. This was a saving grace. Some of the other children at the home were beginning to get into serious trouble for mugging old ladies and beating people up in the street. I was beating people up in the boxing ring, and getting praise and medals in exchange.

The order and discipline that boxing brought to my life also saved me from what would go on to blight the lives of most of the children at St Leonard's in one way or another. I have never been one for alcohol and drugs, although I spent years and years of my working life in and around bars and clubs and various seedy establishments filled with equally seedy characters. I had innumerable opportunities to get into the drug scene, but fortunately I never had any interest. Boxing taught me how to control the violence that was just beneath my surface all the time, and I knew enough to see that taking drugs or getting drunk would threaten the control that had become so important to me.

However, although something good was happening in my life, I was also developing a very nasty streak. For years, I had been a bullied little runt, afraid of my own shadow and convinced that all of the horrible things that Starling and Coral said about me every day were absolutely true. Now that I had developed seriously good boxing skills, I was very ready to do some bullying of my own and more than prepared to bring my boxing skills out of the ring and on to the street. Nobody was going to look at me sideways more than once. I began to feel a little better about myself – but only a little. I was still going home to care workers who told me every day in a myriad of ways that I was stupid and unwanted and unloved.

Because Starling was in charge of the finances, the carers creamed as much money off as they could, and saved a bundle by feeding the majority of the kids rubbish – mostly just bread and margarine with a couple of fish fingers or a spoonful of beans. There never seemed to be enough bread and margarine, and there would literally be fistfights for it. We were growing kids who were hungry all the time, and at mealtimes it was a question of the survival of the fittest. We would just grab all the food we could and stuff it into our mouths as fast as possible. As soon as I was old enough, I got a paper round so that I could fill up on sweets and crisps. Another lifeline was the bottles of milk that milkmen left on people's doorsteps. We stole the milk and any other dairy products that had been delivered to the house-holders and scoffed them on the way to school to fill up, because our breakfast of bread and marga-rine was never enough. I had to fit my paper round in without getting in the way of the work the carers organised for us. They were on to a bit of a scam, getting us to deliver advertising brochures for the local shopkeepers, and keeping our pay to augment their salaries and whatever they could keep from the food budget.

One of the ways Starling kept control in the home was by having a regime whereby the older kids were told that they were responsible for keeping the little ones in order, thus deflecting any responsibility for how this discipline was enacted. When I was little, one of the other kids often gave me a bit of a walloping at Uncle Bill's request. There was a reward system in place. If the older children kept the younger ones under control, they would receive certain favours, such as permission to stay up late and watch television, or an exemption from Uncle Bill's ritual humiliations. Uncle Bill would smile approvingly when one of the little ones got whacked around the head by a bigger kid. Not all the older children wanted to hurt the little ones, although they then got in trouble for not doing what they were told. Although I was a bit of a thug and never hesitated to take on someone my own size or bigger who was having a go at me, as I got older I drew the line at beating up little children and I hated Uncle Bill so much I didn't care about the fact that I was not getting on his good side as a result. I had little enough self-respect as it was, without resorting to hurting the little ones.

In 1975, I was still just thirteen, but I knew what I wanted to do and who I wanted to be like. I idolised Muhammad Ali, who was the reigning hero of the day and a role model I really looked up to. His biography is still the only book that I have ever read from cover to cover and my house is full of as many photographs of him as I can get away with. I even have one from his very early days, signed 'Cassius Clay'. It must be worth about a thousand pounds by now. But I would never sell it; it is one of my most prized possessions.

Muhammad Ali was everything I dreamed of being and the fact that he was black didn't make any difference. In fact, I had grown up with so many black kids that I was not really sure what the difference between us was supposed to be. We were all rejects together. Anyway, there was Muhammad Ali – handsome, strong, gentlemanly and dangerous. He was on television all the time in those days. I never missed a fight and when I saw him being interviewed I hung on every word he uttered, glued to the small black and white screen in the television room. Afterwards, I would lie in bed and revisit the interview, remembering every word and every nuance.

In 1975, Muhammad Ali fought Joe Frazier. Ali got beaten up for fifteen rounds, hit with big swinging hooks over and over again, and in the last round he got knocked down. But he was not going to stay down. Despite the indescribable pain that he must have been suffering, he got up and finished the fight. I have never seen anyone so brave.

But Muhammad Ali was not just brave in the boxing ring; he didn't let anyone in the outside world give him shit either. During the Vietnam War, he had been banned from boxing because he refused to go to Vietnam, on the grounds that he had no problem with the Vietnamese, so why should he want to kill them? This was at a time when prominent black people were getting murdered in the United States. Malcolm X was assassinated. Martin Luther King was assassinated. But Muhammad Ali, he was a survivor and he was brave, even when everyone called him a coward for standing up for what he believed in. He just stood proud and tall and told the rednecks of America, 'No Viet Cong ever called me nigger, and I'm not going to go and kill a yellow man because a white man tells me to.'

Because I wanted so badly to be like Muhammad Ali, I identified with him and decided that I would do my very best to grow up to be like him in every way that I could. He became a real father figure to me, although of course our relationship was completely one-sided. We were both from the underclass – it didn't make any difference that he was black and American and I was neither, because we were both from groups that 'polite society' would have preferred not to exist. He was brave, and I wanted to be as brave as him. He fought on when his jaw was broken and I decided that I would be prepared to do the same thing. He spoke out about what he believed in even when his opinions were unpopular. He was never knocked out or stopped. He never let pain stop him from doing anything. There were times when Muhammad Ali lost fights, but he was always as brave in defeat as he was gracious in victory. Whenever I was in a fight that did not seem to be going well, I would think of Muhammad Ali and I would tell him, and myself, that I would never give up. When I was hurt in the ring, I got back on my feet. When someone was rude to me or belittled me, I tried to think, What would Muhammad do? – although I rarely reacted as graciously as he would have.

Back then, Muhammad Ali was everything I wanted to be. He still is.

After years of hating school, I was finally expelled, to much relief on both sides. The teachers had been violent to me and the other kids for years, and I finally started hitting back, having decided that enough was enough and that I just didn't want to take any more of their shit. It could have been any of the teachers, but on this particular occasion it was someone who had hit me one time too often.

He came at me with the cane, and I laid into him and knocked him out. I had got to the point where I knew that I could throw punches accurately and effectively and this guy was in the wrong place at the wrong time; he also deserved what he had coming to him, which meant that I had no qualms whatsoever about giving him a serious thump. So there he was, stretched out on the floor in front of me, blood trickling from his nose and on to his clean, white cotton shirt, and his mouth and eye swelling where I had hit him. I permitted myself a little smile. It was good to see one of the teachers finally getting what he deserved.

'You'll pay for this, Connolly,' he said weakly, taking a handkerchief out of his pocket and dabbing gingerly at his wounds as he struggled to his feet.

'Fuck you,' I said.

Unsurprisingly, I was called up before the Principal.

'You're out,' he told me. 'You can't hit a teacher! You're lucky that he's not pressing charges. You're lucky that you are not going to serve time for this.'

'Fine by me,' I said. And it was. At the back of my mind, the whole thing had been an exercise in the hope that I would get thrown out because I just couldn't take it any more.

That is how I left school at fourteen, illiterate,

skinny, undersized, bruised and angry. I could not even recite the months of the year. I did not know anything. Nothing at all. Of course, it didn't matter, I felt, because I was going to be a professional boxer, and I would be able to hire other people to do whatever reading and writing needed to be done. For the time being, however, I needed something to do and I needed a way to make some money.

As they had done so many times before, my friends at the boxing club came through for me. They knew a guy called Frank who had a fruit and vegetable stand at Romford Market, and they sorted me out with a job working for him. The job was a relief after the torture of school; I liked it and, although I hadn't been able to do maths at school, I could work out change in my head and performed my duties reasonably well.

Although I was earning money now, I was still officially a minor, and would continue living in St Leonard's for another four years. Every evening, when it was time to go back to the home, my heart would sink.

I knew how to take care of myself, I reasoned, but I couldn't take care of everyone. While all the children at St Leonard's were inclined to be self-destructive, some of the kids were seriously harming themselves. Glue sniffing was rife to the extent that little effort was ever made to hide it, and equally little effort expended on stamping it out. Possibly the care workers figured out that it was probably easier for them to manage the kids when they were confused and off their heads. I remember one of the boys being rushed off in an ambulance because he had gone too far with his glue sniffing and was having trouble breathing. It must have been a terrifying experience for that particular kid, but there was no visible decline in sniffing among the solvent abusers after that. By the time the youngsters at St Leonard's reached fifteen or sixteen, loads of them were smoking marijuana every day, but I don't think there were any hard drugs. There were not all the drugs around then that there are now, for one thing. A little later on, a lot of the glue sniffers would graduate to heroin, which ultimately killed a large number of them. They sniffed glue to try to forget about how unhappy they were, and I am sure that this was also the reason why they took heroin when they were older. For me, violence served the same purpose. I found that I got a real adrenaline high from my bouts in the boxing ring and an even better one from my less regulated encounters on the street.

The combination of fear, deprivation, drugs and general mayhem among the inmates at St Leonard's created a situation in which outbursts of violence among the children and teenagers were a daily occurrence, and the girls were almost as bad as the boys. I had already been carrying a knife with me for several years, and in this respect I was far from unusual. Most of the kids had weapons about their persons at any given time. They had weapons stuffed down the waistband of their trousers or in their socks. They had weapons hidden in the dormitory and all over the garden. They had weapons in their school bags. Often, when I was playing outside, I would find a knife or a bat or a sharpened screwdriver under a bush or secreted behind a drainpipe. We all wanted to be prepared for any occasion, and knowing that there was always a weapon to hand made us feel a bit more in control of our situation.

I will always be grateful for the fact that boxing gave me a way to escape from grim reality and hope for the future. Most of all, it gave me a glimpse of normal family life and, as I passed through my early teenage years, I increasingly realised that the status quo at St Leonard's was not normal and that it was not right. The ordinary teenagers I knew from the boxing club didn't go home to beatings and abuse, but to parents who only punished them when they had actually misbehaved, and who worried about them and cared about them and gave them food that was not just abundant but tasted good too. They even tried to encourage them, and said things like, 'Well done, son.'

Before, my anger had been general and without focus, but now I was angry because of the childhood I had never had and because of the childhoods that were being stolen from my foster siblings at St Leonard's still.

Most of all, I became angry with the adults at St Leonard's, but I also became angry with the Catholic Church. Until I was fourteen, I had attended Catholic school where I had received nothing but hardship. You would go into one class and get caned for giving a smart answer or for looking out of the window, and then you would go into another and the religion teacher would tell you that violence was wrong and to love your neighbour as yourself. And then we were expected to go to confession every week and own up to our sins, in return for which we were given the usual ritual penance to pay. I didn't know the word 'hypocrisy' but I definitely knew what hypocrisy looked like, and I saw it every day in the faces of the good Catholics who were supposed to be teaching us.

Fucking dirty, sanctimonious, hypocritical pricks.

Well, they would all be history when I had made it as a boxing pro. Oh yes, they would be sorry then!

My idea of becoming a professional boxer was a whole lot more than a pipe dream, because I was actually very good at it, and had been boxing competitively since I was thirteen. I was the rising star of the small club I had joined a few years before. I was not the only one. There were some seriously good boxers at the club, some of whom had won major amateur championships. One of the guys at the club, Tommy Butler, was an England boxing coach.

Because we lived in East London, we were boxing with West Ham and the East End of London. I did well. Tommy encouraged me: 'You'll be boxing for England, you know. You really will.'

If the teachers and the caregivers at St Leonard's had always been my tormentors, Tommy was a hero to me. Because he was kind and looked after me and was also tough and manly and did not take shit from anyone, he gave me some idea of how a man was supposed to behave, and I think that his example and my efforts to emulate him helped me to feel protective towards the younger children in care and a bit better about myself. At any rate, I was never attracted to the idea of keeping them in line, the way Bill Starling wanted us bigger ones to do.

As I got better and better, I started to fight at regional level and won many amateur titles. That meant that I was one of the best boxers in the whole region at my weight and age, and well on my way to dominating at national level. This was a real achievement and I acknowledged it, but I still felt that I was no good because that is what I was told every day. This made me work harder. It was a constant quest to feel better about myself – a goal that was still a work in progress.

Without the hope that boxing and my dream of being like Muhammad Ali gave me, it would have been very easy for me to go the way of most of the kids in care, into alcohol and drug abuse, petty criminality and prison. Without my dream that I might be successful one day, I am pretty sure that I would be dead now. Dead, or in prison. Without my dream, most of the things that Uncle Bill and his colleague Auntie Coral said about me would probably have come true. I had learned how to hurt people – badly – but I had also learned how to be disciplined, how to train, how important it was not to abuse my body and how to respect others when they respected me. Boxing taught me how to be a gentleman. But it also trained me in the art of being the best street thug I could be.

Working on the fruit and vegetable stall was good for several reasons. First and foremost, I was not in school any more. That was already great – and, as I planned to become a professional boxer, it didn't matter that I could not read and write. Then, because I was earning my own money now, I could largely decide what to spend it on. I mostly spent it on food. I had been hungry all my life and now I started to make up for it, and more. I was ravenous all the time. I had never been fed properly, so I had no control around food, and I was very physically active because of my boxing, so I just wanted to eat, eat, eat and then eat again. Because of the way I had been brought up, I had no idea what a balanced meal was supposed to entail so I craved the quick fix of sugar, fat, salt and grease. I used to do things like go to Marks and Spencer to buy a pint of double cream, and then open it and drink the lot outside on the street. How wonderful! It slid down my throat the way that dried-up fish fingers and bread and margarine never could. I could not get enough. I had been living on bread and margarine, fish fingers and spam all my life. I had fourteen years of that to cancel out.

I worked quite well for Frank on the stall, but my eyes were always on the goal of becoming a boxer. The job was just to earn me some money in the meantime and Frank was just a decent bloke who treated me fairly. I didn't pay him a great deal of attention one way or another but I think that I did my best to work hard for him when I was at the market. Apart from having to go back to St Leonard's every night, I was quite happy and things were a lot better than they had ever been for me before. I even started to dress well, by the dubious standards of the 1970s, and to take some pride in my appearance. Although I continued to be quite small for my age, I was turning into quite a handsome boy and having some better clothes made me feel good about how I looked. This was very welcome indeed. The kids from St Leonard's were always very badly dressed, because the caregivers used to buy us the cheapest rubbish that they could find. Our clothes were provided from the stores in the home. At school we wore our uniforms and the rest of the time we wore the few clothes we had. I remember having a wardrobe with two tops and two pairs of trousers in it. We were all in the same situation. Now that I had started earning money I really enjoyed going to shops and picking out my clothes and not having to look like just one of the kids from the home. I spent some of my money on high-waist brown trousers with flares and colourful shirts and big, heavy shoes with platform soles. I wore my hair in a fashionable style and started to take more of a focused interest in girls.

I didn't lose my virginity until I was in my later teens, which was really very late indeed by the standards of most of the kids that I knew. The local girl who had the honour of deflowering me was known as the village bike, so she was really the best person for me to lose my virginity to because she was very experienced and knew exactly what to do with a nervous kid who had never been with a woman before. If I had been with another first-timer, it probably would not have worked out as well as it did. I had been to an all-boys' school so I didn't have particularly refined habits around girls and I was anxious to learn more about how to talk to them and how to get them into bed. I hooked up with her at a local pub or club and one thing led to another. I said goodbye to my virginity with no regrets and determined to set about getting some more of the same. We never had a relationship but I didn't look back after that and I went on to be quite successful with women in general. I was good-looking and very fit, both qualities that are appreciated by teenage girls.

My first real girlfriend was a gorgeous girl called Lindsey who was the daughter of a local police sergeant. I met her the way teenagers usually met – just hanging around the local shopping centres and outside McDonald's, which was still relatively new in Great Britain and had not yet lost the shiny newness of America that it seemed to represent. We stayed together for two years. Being with Lindsey was a wonderful experience for me, not just because I had a beautiful, sexy girlfriend and my first real love, but also because her family was kind and normal and both generous and welcoming to me, even though I was a tough, Irish kid from St Leonard's and a bit of a ruffian, to put it mildly. They used to invite me around for dinner, and I got to know Dave and Val, Lindsey's parents, and her sister Carol. This, together with my experiences of the boxing club, taught me a bit about what life is really all about and helped to prevent me from becoming 'institutionalised', which is the name given to the awful, crippling mental condition that destroys the lives of so many of the kids who grow up in care without having any experience of the real world.

I had seen slightly older boys leave the home and flounder straight away, completely unable to cope with reality or even attempt to negotiate the ups and downs of life without someone telling them what to do every step of the way. A lot of them went almost straight to borstal after getting in trouble for mugging old ladies or generally making a nuisance of themselves. From borstal it was a short trip to prison where they quickly learned a few tricks of the trade from the older criminals, and began a career that would see them in prison more often than they were out. For many of these lads, borstal and prison were where they felt most comfortable, and there was certainly a big element of actively wanting to get caught, because life on the outside was just too difficult to deal with. If it wasn't borstal, it was the Army, which is another traditional career move for boys who have grown up on the wrong side of the tracks, have a weak educational background and poor self-esteem; anywhere you didn't have to think for yourself and meals appeared on a metal tray at regular intervals.

In general, many if not most of the kids who

leave care don't have a fucking clue. They have never had to take care of themselves in any way and nobody has ever tried to teach them how to negotiate the maze of life or even basic things such as good manners or how to cross the road safely or a skill that they can sell in the workplace. A lot of them end up back in an institution one way or another very quickly, by which I mean they generally do something stupid and end up behind bars. Many of these angry, bitter unloved young men with no skills and no way of getting on in life tend to commit crimes so idiotic that the police pick them up almost straight away; often before they have even had a chance to enjoy their ill-gotten gains.

One of the kids from my generation at St Leonard's outdid himself by holding up a bookies with a gun and then using the local taxi service as a getaway car. He had called the taxi company beforehand, so, when he came out with his money, the cab was already there, waiting for him. Obviously he was caught almost straight away. It is hard not to assume that he probably wanted to continue being a ward of state for the simple reason that he did not know how to do anything else.

After the first few trips to borstal, that is more or less it for boys like him; they have become confirmed petty criminals who will never be employable and whose lives will never amount to anything. At that point, the very best you can hope for them is that somehow their chaotic sexual encounters don't result in children, because they are probably too sad and too damaged to be proper fathers. This was pretty much the fate that awaited at least one of my older brothers.

When we were kids, we were told by the care workers over and over again that we were institutionalised. This is the term that any analyst looking at this boy's case would surely use about him. It occurred to me recently that, if this was true of the kids at St Leonard's, it was also true of the staff who lived and worked in the children's home. Those who left childcare often went straight into work in another institution, as if no other type of work existed. They had grown so used to being able to boss everyone around and count on a regular pay package from the government that they did not know anything else.

When I was about sixteen, I started working on my tattoo collection. In those days, the skinheads had just started and the first big tattoo I got was of a skinhead with the characteristic shaved head, braces and rolled-up jeans and wearing a skin-tight Union Jack T-shirt. I have often been asked, 'What's all that about? Are you racist?' But what people don't know is that in the very early days, when I got my tattoo, the skinheads were not racist at all. They were fans of 'Oi' music, which was a type of reggae, and the skinheads represented a sort of street movement that originally had both white and black adherents. Later, the whole thing got taken over by British National Party thugs, the way the Hindu Swastika was taken over by the Nazis, and I was left with my tattoo! I often have to explain it to people and it is a frequent source of embarrassment.

Most of my tattoos feature Union Jacks in a variety of settings. One says '100% British Made'. Now, I knew very well that both my parents were as Irish as could be. They had rejected me and handed me over to the tender mercies of the British state. I felt that they must surely have hated me, even though I had only been a tiny baby. I wanted to erase them completely and getting Union Jacks inscribed indelibly all over my body seemed to help a bit. Today, while I don't necessarily remain fond of my many tattoos, I don't feel inclined to have them removed, as this would entail deleting part of my life. Like it or not, they are very much part of who and what I am – they inscribe my history – and I don't feel that I should be ashamed of them.

Another good thing about getting older was that there was much less to fear from Uncle Bill. He tended not to beat up the older children, because there was a risk that they would hit back. He was getting older too, and perhaps all those years of lashing out had given him tennis elbow. Sometimes he did get hit back; I remember my brother Declan lashing out at him and running away. By the time I was sixteen, Uncle Bill would not have dared to come near me. He knew how fit and strong I was, and he must also have had some idea of the anger that was continuously simmering inside me. I was like the stray dog that has been beaten one time too many, always ready and poised to attack. And he knew it. I had shown my potential for violence when Alan Prescott had tried it on with me a few years earlier. Uncle Bill tried again to enlist me to help keep the younger children in line, but, although I had some seriously nasty tendencies, I drew the line there. I had enough self-respect for that. And I certainly was not going to do anything to curry favour with Uncle Bill.

But I wasn't scared of getting into violent situations with kids my own age or older. I was about fifteen the first time I was stabbed. One of the kids at St Leonard's was a black kid who had loads of friends on the outside. A whole bunch of his East End pals had come down to visit one evening and they were outside in the drive making loads of noise and keeping the little ones awake. I went outside to tell them to shut up. I pretty much felt like the little ones' big brother, so that was where I was coming from. I wasn't particularly looking to get into trouble, but I was prepared to do whatever it took to make the East End boys go away. Uncle Bill and Coral were cowering inside, too scared to go out.

Like most bullies, they couldn't cope when there was a risk that they themselves might be confronted.

'What the hell is going on here?' I roared. 'Do yourselves a favour and fuck off home.'

'Says who?' It was a tall black boy, swaggering about with an air of bravado.

'Says me. Fuck off.'

'Are you going to make me?'

'Yeah, I fucking am.'

We squared up against each other for what I assumed was going to be a fist fight. I wasn't afraid of being hit; I was a boxer, after all. The kid struck me a blow and I retaliated by punching him in the head and knocking him to the ground. He fell quickly with a heavy thud. I looked down at him on the floor. He didn't look as though he was going anywhere soon. He groaned and rolled his eyes. I poked him with my foot, but he didn't react.

That's you sorted then, I thought. Good night! I turned and started to walk away. Then, I felt a sensation of warmth spreading across my belly. I looked down. A huge red stain was extending across my midriff. I had thought that I had received a light blow to the stomach, but I had been sliced with a Stanley knife. It wasn't a deep cut, but any stomach wound tends to bleed profusely and this one was no exception. An ambulance was called, and I had to go to hospital to get five or six stitches. Fortunately, the wielder of the Stanley knife had slashed rather than stabbed, so I had not suffered any internal damage. Of course, I went to the hospital on my own as I had on various occasions in the past, clutching a rolled-up towel to my midriff to absorb the blood.

While I waited to be treated in A&E, the police came to take a statement. They acted tough and mean: 'We're not letting a doctor see you until you tell us who it was.'

'I'm not fucking telling you. None of your fucking business. I'm not making any complaints, so why do you need to know?'

'Fine then. You're a tough guy, are you? Then you can just stand there and bleed until you are ready to tell us.'

'Fine.'

I was full of bravado, but I was still bleeding heavily and I was starting to feel woozy. I stood my ground and tried to look as defiant as possible.

Just then, Lindsey's dad, Sergeant White, walked in. Sergeant White was an officer at Barkingside nick in North East London and senior to the policemen who were hassling me. He was outraged by what he saw. Even if I had done something wrong, there was no excuse for not letting me get medical treatment – and in this particular case I hadn't done anything wrong.

'What the hell is going on here?' he roared. 'This boy is the victim in this situation. Leave him alone. Let him see the doctor. You're a disgrace to the uniform!'

I got stitched up and Sergeant White took me back to his house to spend the night. He could not have been kinder, but shortly afterwards Lindsey broke up with me by means of a 'Dear John' on her dad's advice. Even then, I didn't blame him, although my heart was broken and it would take me a very long time to recover. I knew that Lindsey was a sweet girl who didn't deserve to be with a thug like me.

On another occasion, I was hanging about in the street with a bunch of kids while one of the black boys started teasing a couple of geezers at the bus stop. This was in Hornchurch, where the only black kids to be seen were from the home, and everyone knew it.

One of the men turned to me with a grimace. 'You're a nice white kid,' he said. 'What are you doing hanging around with these black bastards?'

I didn't stop to think. I just went up to the guy and knocked him out cold with one right hook. Those kids were my brothers, and brothers stand up for each other! I wasn't going to just stand there and listen to this arsehole be racist. Later, I felt guilty about having hurt an older man, but I still did not understand why he called them 'black bastards' and singled them out for particular abuse. I just didn't get it. Racism didn't make any sense to me then and it still doesn't.

5
THE DAY I DIED

Although I was still not old enough to leave the home, my life was increasingly autonomous. Because Starling knew that the older kids – some of whom were as old as twenty – were generally rather violent characters, he tended to withdraw from them for fear that they would start hitting back. We were responsible for things like doing our own ironing and generally looking after ourselves, and Uncle Bill and the other carers, including Auntie Coral, had as little to do with us as possible. We even bought our own food and cooked it ourselves in the cottage kitchen. When Uncle Bill and other carers did have to interact with us, they generally treated us reasonably well now; at any rate, they didn't want to risk provoking us. After the childhoods that we had experienced, we were all ticking time bombs and it didn't take much to set us off. But, as we all approached the magical age of eighteen, our eyes were fixed on the future, and we didn't want any aggro either. We just wanted to get out like any adolescent kid who doesn't get on with his or her parents.

Auntie Coral did have one very lucky escape from me. One day, I had come home from work and I was cooking something for myself in the kitchen. Coral started to moan at me about something or other and then she started in on her usual litany of complaints: 'You're just a thug; you're one of those stupid, awful Connollys. You'll never amount to anything. You'll be behind bars soon. You'll be in prison all right; you've got absolutely nothing going for you, have you? Big, stupid lout like you.'

'What did you say?'

'You heard me.'

'What did you say?'

Heat rose up through my body until I felt as though I was going to explode. I had been listening to the exact same words from this woman for almost as long as I could remember. I never knew quite why she hated me so much, and I still don't understand it. Auntie Coral wasn't nice to any of the kids, don't get me wrong, but she seemed to reserve special ire for me. Maybe it had something to do with the fact that I had an outside interest in boxing and I wouldn't let her destroy me completely, although she wreaked havoc with my self-esteem, telling me every day that I was a worthless piece of shit who deserved all the crap that the world threw at me.

'You heard me. You're a lout, no more and no ...'

But this time she didn't get to finish her rant. This time, I was ready to fight back. Finally, I couldn't take it any more. I got so hot and angry I could practically feel the steam coming from my ears. My hands tightened on the table until my knuckles were white and the veins were standing out on my arms. My muscles were so tense that they almost hurt. It was a big, heavy kitchen table but I didn't feel its weight in my hands as I picked it up and threw it over with tea and coffee and laden plates on it. I wanted to see Coral squashed underneath it like the wicked witch beneath the house in *The Wizard of Oz*.

The table landed just in front of Coral and she opened her greasy mouth and started to scream. I ran towards her and put my face in front of hers and shouted, 'You fucking slag. I'll rip your fucking head off, see if I don't.'

Auntie Coral did not say anything. She just stood there shaking with her mouth open and her eyes wide. I really wanted to hurt her. I wanted to make her bleed. But, for some reason, I didn't lay a finger on her fat body.

I've got to get out of here, I thought, or I'm going to kill the bitch. I left.

The police were called, as they always were

whenever there was a violent incident of any kind at the cottage, because Starling couldn't deal with the situation that he had helped to create. They all agreed that I had to leave, even though I was still only seventeen and officially a minor. The consensus was that I was too violent and dangerous to be allowed to stay in St Leonard's.

When I was told that I would have to go, I was terribly, desperately upset. In fact, I felt completely bereft. That might seem strange, but, as horrible as St Leonard's was, it was still the only home I had known since I was eight years old, and Bill Starling and the other carers were the closest things to parents that I had ever had.

And, although I had thought that I was looking forward to growing up and making my own way in the world, now I felt as though I was being thrown out of my home and into a desperately unfriendly, frightening world.

Leaving the home at seventeen was very tough. The state was a consistent parent figure; I will give it that. It did not give a shit about society's rejects when we were kids, and it was indifferent to most of us when we left. There was no suggestion of organising an apprenticeship or anything like that. It was a question of: 'You're on your own, mate!' As most of us had no real skills and few if any educational achievements, our chances of getting ahead were very slim, to say the least.

Despite the fact that I had always been so unhappy there, I stayed in the area near where I had grown up. To tell the truth, it did not occur to me to go anywhere else, and nor did I even realise how big the world or even Great Britain was. Young people need a sense of identity. For most of them, this comes from belonging to a family and a community and, knowing that they will always have someone and somewhere to return to, they are free to travel and make their own way in the world. For kids who have grown up in care, those two important sources of identity are not there. Their only identity comes from who they know and where they live. I would have been scared to death at the thought of having to go away from the familiar streets of my home turf. Here, I was a tough little thug who most people disliked – but at least they knew who I was! And that was my sense of identity; being recognised by friends and foe, and having people knowing my name. These were the things that mattered to me.

As always, some of the kids from the home were more equal than others, even on leaving. My erstwhile friend Simon, who had been one of the carers' special friends since the age of thirteen or so, was given a three-bedroom house for himself and his girlfriend when it was time for him to move on. This relative luxury would not prevent Simon from doing himself in, the slow way, by taking heroin until he died some years later, so the 'favourable' attention he received didn't end up doing him any favours. Of course, I do not know any of the details of what Simon had to endure, but I do know that he spent far too much of his childhood holed up in that man's apartment and that he was a troubled youth then and when he eventually left St Leonard's.

Simon and his girlfriend got married when they were still very young and had a family. Throughout their brief married life, right up until Simon died of his heroin habit, his 'carer' kept hanging around all the time, acting as grandfather to their children and telling them that he was the best friend Simon could have, even though he must have contributed substantially to or even been the sole cause of the psychological distress that finally killed him. When Simon died, it was because his veins had collapsed – he had just injected one time too many. One can only imagine what it was that Simon was trying so desperately to forget.

As for me, I remember one member of staff who helped me rather half-heartedly to find my own first bedsit to live in, and after that I was almost completely on my own. A pal of mine, Trevor Schofield, who worked in the local building trade, picked me up in his battered car and drove me to my new place. The fact that Trevor was there for me was a real comfort and a reassurance that I had some friends on the outside who would help me to negotiate a new and unfamiliar world. Now that I was on my own, I started to realise how much I didn't know. I had never had to deal with keys, for instance, and I just could not get used to them. When I was in my first bedsit, I kept losing my keys because I had never had to deal with keys and key rings before.

My first independent home was a grotty room in a young couple's house, just about five miles away from St Leonard's. I remember sitting on the sagging bed in that small room looking disconsolately at the bare walls and thinking, What the fuck am I going to do now?

I unrolled a bedraggled Muhammad Ali poster and stuck it on the wall. I looked at it for inspiration. On this particular occasion, Muhammad didn't come up with the goods. I sat back down again.

I might have been a hard case but I was still only seventeen and there were plenty of moments when I still felt like a little boy in need of more support and help than would ever be forthcoming from a Muhammad Ali poster. Nonetheless, it didn't occur to me to try to renew contact with my parents, although it would probably have been quite easy to find them. I had not seen either of them for years and I rarely thought about them at all, with the exception of the occasional dreams I had about my mother. They came to me unbidden – visions of pumping my fist into her nose, over and over again until all that was left of her face was a bloody, unrecognisable mask. I had had some girlfriends and even one I had loved, and I still remembered Mary with fondness, but in general my opinion of women was very low indeed. Between my mother, who had left me out with the rubbish, and Coral, who had been such a bitch to me ever since I moved to St Leonard's, I had not been given the best examples of feminine kindness.

Although it was difficult, I decided there and then that I would never have anything to do with anyone from St Leonard's again. I would never visit to hear Starling or Auntie Coral telling me what a worthless piece of shit I was, and I would cut myself off completely from all my old friends, including Liam, my oldest and best-loved friend, because even the people I cared about most would remind me of where I had grown up. Although Liam and I had been so close as kids, we drifted apart easily with no backward glances. I left the home before he did and so far as I know he returned to the East End, which must have been where his family came to after they emigrated from Ireland. From the moment we left care, Liam and I didn't have anything to do with each other; nothing at all. I think it was mostly my doing – wanting to wrench myself away from the cesspit I had grown up in, and not letting myself worry about the fact that this also meant not even bothering to say 'goodbye' to my best friend. I will regret the end of our relationship for the rest of my life, far more than any words can express. Perhaps, if I had been in Liam's life, I might have been able to help when he started falling apart in his twenties. The policewomen who called to my house to tell me what had happened called it 'schizophrenia' but that seems like a convenient label to me. Perhaps all Liam needed was someone who understood what he had been through and where he came from. I wish that person could have been me.

As I had a few friends and acquaintances from the boxing club, I did know some people and I quickly found work in the building trade, a traditional area for men who are not afraid of hard work and might not be the best at reading and writing. I was still illiterate and, while my boxing was going well and my trainers assured me that I was full of potential and had what it took to go professional, I wasn't yet earning enough money for me to survive on. Finding a job was quite easy. I was just walking down the street one day when I passed the offices of a local roofing company, walked in and asked for a job. They took one look at me and my taut muscles and gave me work on the spot. The money was much better than what I had been able to earn on the vegetable market, and I quite liked the work which I found fairly easy, as I was very fit and strong as a result of all my boxing and working out in the gym. My employers could not believe how agile I was; I ran about the roofs just like a monkey. Although I was extremely strong, I was also very light and lean and it was easy for me to move around high above the pavement. I also didn't particularly care whether or not I fell off, as I felt that I was quite indifferent to trivialities such as pain and injury or even death. That made me fearless, which is a very useful quality in a roofer. I demonstrated my fearlessness on one of my first building sites when I got crushed between a dumper wheel and a scaffold and came within a whisker of death. The guys I was working with had to pick the scaffold off me. I didn't get put off work though; I didn't care about little things like that.

Bedsit land was a place where the view changed frequently. All of the bedsits were awful, grim places that nobody in their right mind could designate as 'home'. A lot of them were in other people's houses and they didn't really want me or any tenant there; they just wanted or needed the rent money that I gave them. I moved often, packing up my bits and pieces and rolling up my battered Muhammad Ali posters. A lot of the bedsit landlords didn't want their tenants to use the kitchen or bathroom, so it was a question of having a room with a bed in it, pissing rights over the toilet and that was it. I lived on take-outs, fish and chips, kebabs and curries, which I ate on the street or perched on the side of my bed, wolfing them down straight from the bag. Fortunately, I worked so hard physically between boxing and roofing that I burned off all the calories very easily.

Because I was working on the building sites, I came home in the evenings covered in dust and had to wash as best I could in cold water in a hand sink. Once in a while, I would call around to a friend's place for a bath. A better bedsit always seemed to be around the corner, but I never managed to find it. Some people bunked in with each other but I never fancied sharing a house; I wanted to stand on my own two feet. I can't even begin to describe how lonely it used to get in the evenings, lying on the smelly mattress in whatever shithole I was living, staring at the damp stains on the ceiling and waiting for something to happen. But it still never occurred to me to seek out my old friends, because I had decided that I needed to draw a clear line under my past and move on from it. Once in a while, I bumped into Simon, who lived locally, but after a year or so I didn't see him any more either.

Apart from boxing, which was still my passion in life, I think that my saving grace was the fact that I stayed in Essex, which is where I still live today. Because of my involvement in the boxing club and the roots that I had begun to put down when I worked on the fruit and vegetable stall, I had the beginnings of a support network that would eventually serve me well. Most of the kids I grew up with drifted back to the East End, where they had come from in the first place. Back on their home turf and in many cases having renewed contact with their dysfunctional families and friends, it proved impossible for them not to become the thugs and ruffians they had been destined to be since birth. Without a dysfunctional family to return to, I had to build my own network for myself. Gradually, despite everything, I started to become a reasonably personable guy with friends and (though I say so myself) quite an attractive prospect for the ladies who liked their bit of rough. As I had been put on the waiting list for a council flat from when I left St Leonard's, I also had prospects of a limited kind. So, when I wasn't working or boxing, I had a crowd of mates to hang around with. We were a pretty rough and ready bunch and we were always getting into fights, as we were easily offended and quick to lash out and prove that we were not about to let anyone push us around, but we were also genuinely fond of each other and helped each other out whenever we could. I especially remember Peter and Sam – Psycho Sam as we used to call him, and with good reason. We were all young fellows who worked together, ate packets of chips together, went down the pub together and got into fights and aggro together. Between the mates I had in the boxing club and the friends I met on the building sites who were all from Dagenham, I built up a good crowd. We didn't necessarily talk about anything deep and meaningful but we became quite close in our rough way.

I was one of the smallest guys in the group, and, because I was so light, it was impossible to tell how strong I was just from looking at me. This was a frequent source of entertainment to the gang, and one of our games was to go round the local pubs and invite all the tough guys to have arm-wrestling matches with me.

'You're fucking joking,' they would say when they saw me, 'a skinny little runt like you? I'm not going to wrestle you; I don't want to hurt you! Do yourself a favour and clear off.'

'Scared, are you?' I would say. 'Don't want to risk it? Bit of a girl, are you?'

Well, they wouldn't put up with that; not even from a skinny little bloke like me. And then, because I put in so many hours a week training, I beat them all, knocking over the beefy arms of those eighteen-stone men as if they were so many weaklings. We used to make quite a bit of money doing that, and we would always invest it wisely – in more beer.

My boxing career was going famously. I was boxing in competitions and winning everything. Earlier on, I had lost a few matches and had become a little disillusioned but I just started working harder, and then it was as though nothing could stop me. It seemed that I couldn't stop winning and that no matter what I did I was almost always bound to come out on top. Now everyone was taking me seriously as someone who could really go professional and make it. I even began to respect myself a little. Whenever I got knocked down, I always came back fighting, always with Muhammad Ali in mind – never give up.

My first car was a Cortina which I drove without a licence or insurance. Because I didn't know how to drive properly, I had an accident and wrote it off and found myself up in front of the local magistrate. It took me a few minutes to realise that the person who was overseeing my case was Alan Prescott. I had not seen him since I left St Leonard's. He was easy on me; I got a suspended sentence and a small fine.

I finally got a council flat when I was about twenty-four, after six or seven years of moving from one bedsit to another. It was good timing, because the last bedsit I had been in was a right dive. The landlady wouldn't let me wash in the bath, because she didn't want me using her precious hot water, and as I was coming home filthy from the building sites, I was very meticulous about my personal hygiene, and I hated not being able to wash every day after work. The new flat was just a simple council affair with no bells and whistles but I kept it very clean and tidy and was extremely house proud for a young man in his twenties. Having grown up in a children's home where if you left a possession lying around for more than a minute or two someone nicked it, I have always been a very orderly person. I had a place for everything and everything was in its place in my new flat. I also had a knife tucked tidily into every corner so that I would be ready to defend myself in any eventuality. I arranged the furniture so that, wherever I was sitting, I would never have my back to a door or window.

There were eight people living in my block and before the first year of my tenancy was out I had knocked out about four of them because they were scum and they deserved it. I won't go into all the details, but just to give you one example, the guy who lived in the flat opposite me was a drunk who would come home at four in the morning and find himself locked out because he was too wasted and too stupid to realise the key was in his own pocket. Eventually he would start hammering the shit out of his own door trying to get in and shouting, 'Let me in!' even though he lived alone. Between him and the drug dealer and the guy running prostitutes, I was not exactly in very salubrious company.

Still, some things were going very well.

I was known among my mates for being particularly lucky with women, but things didn't always go exactly according to plan. One night, I had been out clubbing in East London with my pal Psycho Sam and the rest of the boys from Dagenham. As usual, it didn't take me long to pull a good-looking bird who, for the purposes of this book, I'll call Sophie. Sophie and I saw each other for a while, but a month or two into our relationship I had a rather painful experience with my new girlfriend. Sophie still lived at home with her parents. One day, we were messing around on the living-room floor, aware that her Mum and Dad might come back at any moment. In those days, I went commando. I never wore any underwear – I didn't see the point. On this occasion, my lack of underwear had provided quick and easy access to what I saw as a very important element in my relationship with Sophie. Sophie was on top of me, and I still had my trousers on, with the zip down.

When we heard a key in the door, Sophie and I both hurried to cover up. Sophie jumped up and, in the process, a hook on her clothes got caught in my zip and pulled it up right over my erect penis, catching it in its teeth. Years later, I saw the film *There's Something About Mary* and felt the pain all over again. I was in agony, and there wasn't any way of getting the zip down without making matters even worse.

'You've got to get out of here,' Sophie whispered. 'Mum's going to come in here any time now.'

I ran into the downstairs loo, eyes smarting with

the pain, and did my best, but that zip wasn't going anywhere. I could hear Sophie and her mother chatting in the lounge. Sophie was trying to buy me time so that I could get myself sorted. But that wasn't happening.

After about half an hour of some of the worst pain I had ever experienced, we were forced to admit my predicament to Sophie's mum.

Her mum had a look and kept a straight face. 'We'd better call the emergency doctor. You can't stay like that for long. What if you got gangrene?'

Gangrene! I didn't like the sound of that.

When we called the doctor, making a poor job of stifling his laughter, he advised me to get myself to A&E. I didn't like the sound of that, either.

'Give it one last go,' I suggested to Sophie and her mum. 'Maybe we can get it off and I won't have to go into the hospital.'

'All right then.'

So now, my girlfriend and her mum were both down on their knees in front of me trying to pull down the zip, while I bit my lip and tried not to swear in front of my girlfriend's mum.

'I've got an idea,' her mum said. 'I'll get a pair of scissors and cut the zip out of the trousers. Perhaps then it will be easier to pull it down.'

I closed my eyes while she brandished the gleaming scissors around my crotch. No man likes to see blades flashing around that particular area of his body, but she managed to accomplish the procedure. This didn't improve matters much, however. Now I was standing stark bollock naked in my girlfriend's mother's lounge with a zipper hanging off my knob. Even with all the pain I was in, I could see that I must look ridiculous. Even Sophie had succumbed to laughter now, as she went upstairs to find me a pair of tracksuit bottoms to wear so that we could go to A&E without creating a scene.

'What seems to be the problem?' the admissions nurse asked me when I arrived.

'Well,' I explained, 'I have a zipper attached to my knob and I need to have it removed.'

'You what? Give us a look!'

I could see that I wasn't getting any sympathy here. I wasn't getting any discretion either. Along with the laughter, she raised her voice and explained what was going on to her colleagues, who responded with hilarity and rushed over to inspect me. Then I heard a familiar voice calling my name. I looked around and, just my luck, there were some people I knew sitting in A&E, all enjoying the show.

A long and very uncomfortable wait ensued and finally I heard my name called. I was whisked off by a very camp young male nurse who proceeded to lay me down, inject my penis with anaesthetic, cut the zip off and stitch me up. After the procedure, he sympathetically dabbed me with cotton-wool balls soaked in disinfectant.

'Don't worry, love,' he said consolingly. 'You'll be right as rain very soon and we'll have you back in action.'

I heard a snort and looked up to see that Sophie had abandoned all pretence of sympathy by now.

For weeks afterwards, I sported a penis swollen to twice its usual size and black and discoloured with all the bruises. I made the most of it, of course, and showed it off to anyone I thought might be interested and quite a few who probably were not.

And ever since then, I have never gone without my pants!

The male nurse was right, too. Before long, I was back in action, both in terms of getting off with birds, and getting into frequent, bloody fights.

Despite my boxing success and my newfound ability to make friends, I was always scared. Scared that everything that Bill Starling and Auntie Coral had said about me was true. Scared that my achievements in boxing didn't really count for anything and that one day they would all be taken away. Scared that I would find myself in a situation in which I couldn't take care of myself.

And then, one day, quite suddenly, I stopped being scared. I had always been one to get involved with fights, and in one of those fights I was stabbed quite badly. It wasn't like the superficial flesh wound the first stabbing had left me with but a real, deep stab where the knife had penetrated my skin and plunged right into my abdominal cavity. I remember experiencing it as a strange sort of joy, a wordless ecstasy. I put my hand to the warm flow of blood and realised that, although I was going to need medical attention, I was OK. I was going to live. I had been hurt, but they had not been able to do me any lasting damage.

Wow, I thought. That's it. I've been stabbed in the gut and I am still here. It doesn't even hurt as much as I expected. There was never anything to be scared of.

From that moment on, I was never frightened of anything, and I resolved that, from then on, I would never let anything or anyone stand in my way. Now, far from running away from violence, I actively sought it out and, because of the circles I was moving in, it was never difficult to find. Not only was I not scared any more, but I also wanted to prove to myself that I would never be scared again and that I had effectively killed off the frightened little boy I had once been.

Every time an opportunity for me to be violent presented itself, I embraced it wholeheartedly and joyously. Whenever I felt that someone deserved to be hurt, I was more than happy to make sure that he got what he deserved. If I had a spot of bother while I was driving, I would get out of my car, pull the other driver from their vehicle and beat the crap out of them, driving away only when they had been reduced to an abject heap of snot and tears. Whenever anyone wanted to fight with me, I was delighted to give them that opportunity. If they were asking for it, who was I to say no?

Fuck it, I thought. What have I got to lose? I am just going to do what I want to do. Because I hated myself so much, I was always challenging myself and setting myself up for a fall. When I went out, I would look for the biggest, craziest guy and effectively say, 'Come on then, come and shoot me and we'll see who comes off worst.' They were always perfectly satisfied to oblige, until they realised that they had bitten off more than they could chew – and by then it was too late!

From having been a frightened child right up until my early twenties, I suddenly became a raving maniac with a death wish. That was my strength: if you are fighting someone and you are willing to die and they are not, you are going to win. I was willing to die in a fight, to stab or be stabbed, to shoot people and to do whatever it took. I didn't care if I lived or died and that made me utterly invincible. Whenever I got into a fight and found myself looking into the other man's eyes, what he saw looking back at him were the eyes of a person ready and willing to die. There is nothing more terrifying. That was who I was in those days of twenty and more years ago.

Some of the people I fought with were bullies, and I like to think that most of them deserved what they got because if I hadn't beaten the crap out of them they would have done it to me or, worse, to someone who was less able to stand up for himself. As my reputation as a fighter grew, my friends and their friends would give me a ring whenever anyone had been giving them a hard time, and I would happily go and sort it out for them. The aggressors would pull out knives or bats or whatever and threaten me. So far as I was concerned, the more violent and dangerous they were the better, and the more I liked it. The nastier my opponent, the more reason I had to batter him until he was black and blue. I got stabbed and bitten repeatedly, but it was all water off a duck's back to me and, every single time I was badly hurt and survived, it just strengthened my resolve never to back down and my conviction that there was little if anything that anyone could do to seriously damage me.

The trouble was that not everyone I beat up deserved it because I was always very quick to put up my fists, and ever reluctant to negotiate before things turned nasty. So what did that make me? I liked to think that I was standing up for myself and for people who couldn't stand up for themselves, but the fact was that I was becoming as bad as the bullies.

Nothing mattered anyway, because I was on my

way to becoming a boxing champ. And then I would have respect in spades and I was going to be earning ten grand a fight, which also meant that I would have all the women I wanted. Even if I didn't become an international champ, I knew that I would be able to make a decent living as a middleweight; that was my plan B.

Then, when I was about twenty-four, I fell off a roof, ending my plans to become a professional boxer once and for all and taking out plans A and B in one fell swoop, and probably plans C, D and E as well.

What happened was this: I was working on a steeply pitched roof with no scaffold, on a roof ladder that was hooked over the apex of the building and lying flat against the tiles. Because the roof was so steep, the ladder wasn't secured properly and, when it slipped, I ran on the spot like Wile E. Coyote until I fell the seventy feet or so to the ground. My fall was broken by a glass door that the plasterers working in the house had left outside leaning against the wall, and I tore through it on my way to the ground, almost severing my arm and slicing my right hand in half right through the middle. I landed heavily on the ground, surrounded by shards of glass.

I remember the incident very well. I didn't feel any pain at first, just some shock from the impact. I managed to sit up and tried to assess the situation. It all felt quite unreal. The objects around me seemed to be more highly coloured than they should have been, but otherwise everything seemed to be quite normal.

I'm OK, I thought. I'm all right. Just got a bit of a bruise. I got to my feet and tried to run away. I managed to take a few steps. This was the worst thing I could have done, as my arm was hanging by a thread and one of my lungs had been punctured through the back. The motion made the blood pour thickly from my severed arteries. I started to run. All the other guys started chasing me. 'Paul, what the fuck are you doing, mate? You've got to sit down. You've been badly hurt.' They grabbed me and lowered me to the ground as gently as they could. Someone called an ambulance.

What's this? I thought. They put me sitting in a puddle. What the fuck are they playing at? And it's all warm...

I heard somebody retching and looked around. A young bloke who had only recently started working on the site was vomiting up his lunch. Most of it landed on me. I didn't care.

I looked down. The puddle I was sitting in was my own blood and the stain was rapidly spreading across the ground as it merged with my colleague's thrown-up lunch.

Oh, I thought. I'm bleeding...

I was technically dead by the time I reached the hospital.

They managed to bring me around by hooking me up to the machines and pumping me full of someone else's blood. The doctor asked my sister Anne for permission to amputate my hand, as she was the only relative he was able to contact. Fortunately, she did not give it. Now, my hand is missing a finger and some of its functionality, but I would rather have it than not.

When I was together enough for the doctors to talk to me, they explained that they had been able to bring me back from the dead because I was so young and so fit. I could not have been fitter, in fact. I had been training every day, so when they filled me up with someone else's factor A and hoped for the best I was better able to handle it than most.

I had survived the fall, but my boxing career had died. I was never going to be a boxing champion now. I was not even going to make a decent living as a middleweight. My arm was never going to be its old self. That meant that I was just one more illiterate, belligerent, problematic person.

I weighed up my choices. There weren't many.

But then something fantastic happened.

I had to have physiotherapy and all sorts of treatments before I was well enough to go back to work and, in the course of the treatments that I received, I realised that my boxing training had taught me more about physiology and nutrition than most of the healthcare workers I was meeting seemed to know. That meant that I might be able to find some sort of a job in a related area. Perhaps, after all, there was also a plan F.

The biggest problem I faced now was the fact that I couldn't read or write to save my life.

6
GETTING SERIOUS

I was still covered in a roadmap of angry red scars when I went to night school to learn how to read and write, having roundly failed to do that when I was younger. The difference was that now I actually wanted to learn, because I could see that I had no choice. No glittering future as a boxing champ lay ahead of me now. And I wasn't stupid. I knew that with my injuries but without a proper education I would have few opportunities to get on. I knew that not learning to read and write at this point would make it more than likely that most of Auntie Coral's predictions for me would come true. I knew that illiterates generally end up at the bottom of the heap, and the bottom of the heap is not a place where I wanted to spend much time.

Going back to school in my twenties is by far the bravest thing that I have ever done, because only someone who has been in my position knows how mortifyingly embarrassing it is to be unable to read and write; skills that most seven-year-olds have already mastered. I had to summon up hundreds of times more courage than I had ever needed going into a boxing fight or squaring up against someone on the street. Going into the office to arrange the classes was awful, but thank God I did it, because I hate to think of the alternative.

The night school was funded by the government, which was finally doing me a good turn after having participated in my awful childhood by appointing the worst guardians ever. It took me about a year to learn how to read and write to a reasonable level and it was the best thing I had ever done. I still can't spell very well – my son Harley, who, at the time of writing has just completed his reception year in school, is rapidly overtaking me – but technology has caught up with me in the form of computers and their much-appreciated spellcheckers. I took some computer classes as well as literacy classes. I loved using computers because of the underlying logic and because writing on the computer meant that I could check my spelling and that my abysmal handwriting did not matter. We were also taught basic numeracy skills, which I needed almost as much. For light relief, I started shagging a bored housewife who was about ten years older than me who was taking the course out of boredom or perhaps in the hopes of meeting a young stud like me. I did not mind doing her the favour, particularly as she did not expect anything else of me.

It might sound mean, but a lot of the other men and women doing the adult literacy course were real retards who were never going to be able to get to grips with what they were studying, because they simply did not have the necessary grey matter. It was wrenching for me to have to sit with them knowing that I was intelligent and that I still had the same problems that they did. This added to my embarrassment, as did the fact that many of the teachers treated us all as dumbasses and seemed to have very low expectations for us all, without exception. They tried to be nice, but it came over as condescending and it was obvious that most of them assumed that none of us had much between our ears. In most cases, these assumptions were correct but, despite my low self-esteem, I did know that I had it in me to conquer what had always defeated me at school. I gritted my teeth and determined to continue. I knew that I had no choice.

There was, however, one lady, Grace, who was very kind and generous of spirit and seemed to realise how badly I wanted to learn and that I had the capacity to do so. I will always be very grateful to her.

'Look,' Grace said to me. 'This is how it works. If you apply yourself and do your best, I can help you, and you will be able to learn quickly. It is not as difficult as it seems at first and you are more than ready for it.'

Grace helped me outside class too and my proudest moments were when I found myself beginning to read the signs in shop windows and headlines in newspapers without too much effort, just like an ordinary adult person.

As soon as I had acquired a reasonable standard of literacy, I started to study for a gym instructor's qualification, a Fitness for Industry (FFI) certification so that, even if I could not become a professional boxer, I could work in an area that had always interested me. Because I had seen a lot of gaps in the knowledge of the physiotherapists and other professionals who had helped me get well, I felt that there was a need in the market for someone like me, who knew about the practical aspects of health and fitness. Because I was proud and determined to be self-sufficient, I took jobs to pay for the training.

My body had healed, by and large, and I was still very fit and strong despite my injuries so I got jobs as a doorman for nightclubs. As a doorman, I was quickly given the nickname 'Fingers' because of the finger that my right hand was missing ever since I fell off that roof. The tradition of giving doormen nicknames is as old as the profession. Most doormen go by these monikers rather than their real names so that, if a job goes bad, they can scarper and nobody will be able to trace them, because their real name is unknown. I understood the logic behind the tradition, but didn't appreciate my nickname, because 'Fingers' is also a label attached to pickpockets, and I had never been involved in crime, petty or otherwise.

Because the money I was able to make on the door was not quite enough, I also did a bit of mini-cab driving on the side. Mini-cab driving was a pleasant enough way to make some money and pass the time, and it also offered other attractions in the form of the many women passengers who would hire the cab to take them home after a night out with the girls and then invite me up to their place to give them a good seeing to. Women are reputed to be the more retiring sex but, from what I saw, this often is not the case at all. I was young, very fit and handsome with my thick black hair and I was usually happy to oblige, seeing this as an attractive perk of what could otherwise be quite a boring job. I didn't leave the meter running.

When I passed my first qualification, I got distinction for anatomy and physiology. The notes at the bottom said, 'If this was a spelling test you would have failed but luckily enough it's not.'

I was getting somewhere, and finally I began to feel like a bit less of a loser, but my passion for physical fitness was not earning me enough money yet. That still came from the cab driving and, increasingly, from providing security at nightclubs and other venues. Once again, all those years that I had spent boxing stood me in good stead, and, even if the arm that I had injured was not as strong as it used to be, I still had two fists and I knew how and was not afraid to use them. I was a highly trained aggressor who knew all about technique, and I was also a vicious thug with an inferiority complex and an entirely justifiable chip on my shoulder – an explosive combination.

And I still liked hurting people when I felt that they had it coming to them. God, did I like to do that!

As people got to know me on the door, my reputation as someone who was more than able to stand up and fight grew and I started to attract the attention of the sort of men who needed people like me; people who were not afraid to hit first and ask questions later. Nowadays, the area of door and security work is much more regulated in every aspect. By comparison, back then it was like the Wild West. I welcomed every single opportunity to expose myself to violence, and each time I was involved in a confrontation and survived, I became more confident, happier and less like the frightened child I had always been. In those days, doormen were mostly recruited by word-of-mouth. There was a sort of informal network of built-up guys who spent their days in old-school sweat gyms and their nights in black tie on the doors. They were much the same crowd as the ones I had grown up with – the ones who had managed not to end up in borstal, and some who had and who had come out stronger as a result.

Because we were all East End guys, we mostly worked in the East End, but occasionally we did West End gigs too. Whereas the East End was full of difficult people – the usual blacks, Irish, gypsies and general trouble-makers and ne'er-do-wells – the West End was more champagne Charlies and quite upmarket. The West End had its own problems, but they usually did not involve street fights. The East End often offered scenes from hell and, as I was frequently the only white doorman, and the smallest doorman, I saw it all.

One gig I had for a few months was at a club I'll call the Jungle (not its real name), which is a well-known black club in East London. By the time I was working there, it was a massively popular nightclub with jungle music and hordes of drugged-up partiers out for a good time. A good mate of mine was the head doorman, and he was working with Leroy, an equally tough character. Leroy was tough but even he could not deflect bullets. He was shot and killed while I was working at the Jungle. The promoter of the venue had been dealing drugs, and had fallen foul of some drug dealers one night.

They were pissed off because he owed them money. I was working on the door with a big guy called Dexter, who I really liked – everyone liked Dexter. We were expecting trouble, so we were all wearing bulletproof vests and keeping our eyes open so that we would be ready to deal with the tricky situation that we were anticipating. When the dealers turned up, they tried to get into the club, but of course we could not let them. They were understandably upset, and immediately pulled out their guns and started waving them around. We picked them up and threw them out, but one of them came right back and shot Leroy. The bullet ricocheted off Leroy's elbow and went into the side of the vest into his heart, killing him straight away. It was just bad luck that it was Leroy, because it could have been any one of us, and he was massively unfortunate that the bullet ricocheted, because his vest should have been able to absorb the blow.

You might think that the last thing that anyone would want to do after that was go back to working on the door, but the rest of us felt that it would be the right thing to do. We were determined not to be scared off, because we didn't like to think of scumbags of the sort that had killed Leroy getting away with it.

One other night, I was away from one of the doors I usually worked on when another doorman was killed. It was a similar situation. A bunch of tough black guys had turned up from South London and had been refused entry into the club for some reason. The door was slatted, saloon-style, and these guys shot the doors out, took out the window, put their guns through it and unloaded an automatic pistol into the foyer, hitting about ten people. Nobody was ever caught for this crime. The only description received for the guy who had unloaded his pistol was that he was small, black and wearing a hoodie. He could have been one of hundreds of thousands and to the best of my knowledge he was never identified. Chris, the doorman, was one of the people killed and, although I did not know him well at all, I did take note of his death, as we all did, because it could have been any one of us. But none of these things made me scared, because I was fearless, not because I believed that nothing could happen to me but because I really did not care if I got shot and killed. I never did heroin, but I imagine that similar sentiments must be felt by anyone with the habit; I know it could kill me, but who really gives a fuck? Not me, mate.

Who needed drugs when there was a chance of getting killed on any given night at work? Knowing that was my high, right there.

Soon I moved on from just doing door work to private, close-protection jobs for some very serious people who also had lots of wealthy clients, Arabs and foreign dignitaries, all of whom needed bodyguards to take care of them when they visited London. This was very lucrative work for everyone involved and a real change from the environment I was coming from, and I felt that it would open the doors to some real money for me. I was correct in this assumption.

My break came when I was working in London's West End, in a Jewish neighbourhood with a lot of very wealthy residents. I was at a nightclub I'll call Charlie's, which catered to a rather moneyed clientele and presented itself as a very exclusive establishment with a dress code and an entry policy to match. This was the late 1980s and there was cocaine everywhere – it went with the Lycra dresses and the big hair – and it went up the noses of a lot of Premier League players, models and ex-public school boys rolling up in limousines.

A friend of mine ran the door at Charlie's and he invited me to work for him. He told me that not all the money that exchanged hands in the club was legitimate, because there were plenty of drugs floating around, but that wasn't really my concern. I would be there to take care of the punters and to do my best to make sure that nobody got hurt and, so far I was concerned, if people wanted to get off their faces on cocaine that was nobody's business but their own.

I had been used to working in dives where I spent

my nights taking guns away from irate Irish, Scots, blacks, gypsies and regular London geezers and breaking up fights every five minutes, so working the door in a more upmarket establishment was a nice change and a bit of a rest, and it did not make any difference to me whether the punters were sticking cocaine up their noses or not. I had grown used to working for joints where the customers regularly invited the doormen to fight it out. The only way to deal with the dregs of society who turned up was to give it to 'em proper. It was the only language they understood and, if you did not stand up to them, they did not respect you. If you did not beat them to a bloody pulp, they beat you, so it was an easy choice to make. Going to work, it was never a question of whether or not there was going to be some violence, but of how much, and how long it was going to take to quell it.

This West End gig was almost restful in comparison. There was rarely any violence at all, and when there was it was just a little scuffle between a couple of toffs who really did not want to get blood on the expensive shirts they had just picked up on Savile Row. We would take it out the back where they would take a few pops at each other to save face and nobody would ever be any the wiser. The clients were generally nicer here, and a lot of celebrities turned up, which lent a certain amount of glamour to the job.

There was a good rapport among the various doormen at Charlie's and I worked there for quite a long time and grew friendly with the other men. We bonded in a variety of ways. One year, for example, we had a competition to see which of us could shag the most women in twelve months. Because I had a history of success with women, I felt that I was in with more than a sporting chance. We all took the challenge very seriously, and at the end of the year we organised a bona fide ceremony with an Olympic-style podium and bronze, silver and gold medals. It was hilarious. Steve, who was a dead ringer for Tom Selleck as Magnum P.I., came first with forty; I came second and took silver with thirty-eight; and the bronze medal was shared by Billy Big Arms and Nicky No Neck who – for obvious reasons – couldn't both fit on the third-place podium at the same time!

Although there was much less aggro at Charlie's than at some of the other places I had worked, because I was small for a doorman, if anyone ever did want to pick on someone, they chose me. They lived to regret that. Because I didn't weigh twenty stone they tended to seriously underestimate me. I looked smaller than I actually was, too, because I was usually standing next to behemoths. One of the doormen at Charlie's, John (not his real name), was a big guy who was a bit of a bully and most of the doormen tried to avoid John because he was a massive dickhead, basically, with the emphasis on 'massive'.

One night, John was off work and in the club. Of course, he got drunk and as inevitably as night follows day he started to cause trouble. This oversized moron was threatening the barman and harassing women by putting his hands up their skirts and abusing their boyfriends.

The bar was equipped with a red light that went off when a panic button was pushed and, when that happened, we had to get into the bar quickly and deal with the situation. The guy I was working with pretended not to see the red light, because we all knew what sort of reputation the drunken bully had and most of the doormen were scared of John. But I went down, because I wasn't scared. I had been stabbed and beaten so many times by now – what difference did one more time make? Now, John was built like a tank, so fearless or not I had a moment of relief when he left the club by himself. But then he walked straight back in again, because the doormen were too afraid to stop him.

Now I knew that it was my time to shine.

I went and stood in front of John and looked up at his red face. I was standing two steps up from him, but he was still towering over me. 'Where are you going, mate?'

'I'm going inside.' He belched beer fumes down on to me.

'No, you fucking ain't.'

'Says who?'

'Me. Get out, mate. Time to go home.'

'Fuck off, you little prick.'

I knew I didn't have the luxury of time to decide what to do so I hit John with a straight right hand and knocked the gigantic fucker out with one punch. He keeled over like a felled mountain gorilla and lay there sweating and twitching on the tiled floor. It took four of us to lift him up and drag him outside. It was like a scene from *Gulliver's Travels*.

Because Charlie's was a respectable establishment, the police were called, and I was sure that I was going to get nicked, because someone was going to have a very sore head in the morning.

Fortunately for me, John was so embarrassed about having been laid flat by a bloke of about half his weight that he didn't tell the coppers. But my colleagues told everyone they knew, and my reputation and prestige grew exponentially until guys I didn't even know were coming up to me on the street and shaking my hand, saying, 'Well done, mate!'

I could tell you that I did not care what other people thought about me in this particular case but I would be lying; I was delighted and, the way I felt right then, the bigger, tougher and harder they were, the more ready I was to take them on. What did I have to lose? I lived in a shitty council flat. I had no wife, no kids, no loved ones, few real friends and nobody to care about or to care for me.

This was when I came to the attention of men who had a need for private security, including a lot of ex-military types. Often it was a case of people who had to carry a lot of bank bonds or cash from one place to another, and they needed protection. I was more than qualified to provide it.

Now that I was a known and celebrated quantity on the street, I also did a lot of private security work taking care of Arab businessmen visiting London. These gents are Muslims so they are not supposed to drink and they are not supposed to run around with loose women, so of course they do both things as often as possible whenever they visit decadent England where anything goes. They love parties, sex, drugs, booze and general rock 'n' roll and they need people to protect them as they trip about from one nightclub to the next. These wealthy Arabs only go to the finest places in London, and the upmarket establishments are willing to pay handsomely to make sure that their VIP guests are well looked after.

I did not care what my rich Arab friends did with their personal lives and I was happy to provide protection for the generous sums that I was offered. Girls and drugs were on offer too, but I had never had any trouble getting girls on my own and drugs still did not interest me. The job was a doddle compared to working the doors. The clients would go and party in exclusive bars, or in the VIP areas of fancy clubs about town. My job was, firstly, not to let anyone know that I was there and, secondly, to take care of the money that they were carrying with them, arrange for a driver to take them to the airport or do whatever it was that they needed. Because I wasn't an enormous man, I was often picked because I didn't attract attention, which was appealing to people who wanted to keep a low profile.

Because my Arab wards were rich and fancily dressed and perfumed and not generally shy about flashing their money about, they often aggravated the rest of the drinkers and party-goers because the girls were all over them like flies on honey, ignoring Joe Bloggs in his best shirt and cheap cologne for the richies in their Bentleys and Rolls-Royces. Sometimes Joe Bloggs would take a pop at one of them and would have to be bodily removed before trouble broke out. Then, angry, he would turn on whoever happened to be in his vicinity and take his rage out on them instead. Fights were frequent and bloody, the way they tend to be when jealousy and male egos are involved. You could understand it a little; there they were, the ordinary men, standing in a queue for hours to get into the hottest new nightclub, when these rich visitors would pull up in their massively expensive cars and walk past the queues and into the clubs with their own private security and any pretty girl they wanted ready to drop her knickers whenever they clicked their fingers. They had their own areas inside with their own champagne and the best cocaine money could buy. Money talks.

So who the fuck did they think they were?

That was the way people felt about them. I could sympathise, to an extent, but it wasn't my job to be understanding. I had to look after my foreign friends and, if that meant breaking a few noses along the way, so be it. I was glad to oblige.

London is a city that has everything. There are rich people, poor people, good people and bad people. There are honest people, white-collar crooks and petty criminals. There are also a lot of people who fall pretty much across the whole spectrum. Increasingly, my job was to provide security to the sort of individuals who really needed it, because they had plenty of enemies.

Soon my confidence grew so high that not only was I not frightened, but I also became a serious bully. I enjoyed seeing the fear in the eyes of an adversary just before I punched him out or knocked him against the wall. I liked the sight and smell of the blood running out of his broken nose and down his face. I laughed when he pissed his pants out of fear. I liked it all. I was always the smallest doorman but I was also the fiercest. What I was saying each and every time was: 'Right: I have been frightened all my life. I've been bullied all my life. I've had enough. You're the toughest guy in here; let's do it.'

Oh, the fun I had. There are too many examples to relate, but I can give you some.

On one occasion, I was working at the Channel Club in London when I irritated some drug dealers. I had taken some drugs from the wrong dealer and I refused to give them back. This fella had some serious friends, and they arranged for a drive-by an hour or so later to show that they were not happy. There were six of us on the door, and when they pulled the gun on us we all tried to get through the door and got stuck on our way, like in a comedy scene in an old slapstick film. They fired at us but it was just buckshot, which stung more than hurt – and anyway the bulletproof vests took care of most of it.

A few nights later, I had to evict a troublemaker from the club. I had him in a headlock in my arm when he twisted around and bit a chunk out of my side. You've got to keep your tetanus shots up to date in jobs like that.

A few months later again, I was working the door at a rough place in East London. I had to throw out a troublemaker and take his gun away from him. This was the sort of lowlife who might really hurt someone, so disarming him was a priority. It might have been a rough joint, but that didn't mean that the owners wanted any of their customers to be hurt. This savage waited all night for me with his screwdriver at the ready, and when I came out he ran at me with it and stabbed me. I was hurt, obviously, but he came off very much second best, because I just grabbed him in a headlock and ran him into some nearby railings so hard that I fractured his skull. I heard it crunch; I was happy to. It was music to my ears. I did not feel even remotely sorry for him when he started to cry like a little girl or when his jeans suddenly darkened with piss. I even liked the metallic scent of his fresh blood in the cold night air.

When the police came, I was bleeding from my stomach and more or less holding my guts in with my hands to stop them from spilling all over the pavement. I had not been all that badly wounded, but you can't be too careful. I told the coppers what had happened and they nodded knowingly. 'Look, mate, go and get sorted out and we'll say we found him like this.'

The London police know the way the world works and they don't mind playing the game.

Yes, I was on a roll. And despite or perhaps even because of my achievements in those areas where violence is king, I was having a great deal of success with women, especially women in uniform. I had a succession of policewomen girlfriends who seemed to be very turned on by the notion of dating a guy from the wrong side of the tracks, a guy who knew plenty of people on the wrong side of the law.

Traditionally, coppers don't particularly like door-men, which meant that I was forbidden fruit. I think that I was attracted to the fact that they were strong women with authority who were not afraid to wield it. One after another, my girlfriends during this period of my life were women who came home and had to hang up their blue uniforms before getting dolled up to face the night.

As a result of my various injuries – most of which were much less exotic than getting a zip stuck on my knob – I often had to have tetanus injections, stitches and general patching up. I have lots of scars to this day, reminding me of some events that I am proud of, and others that I would rather forget. And while I wouldn't say that I enjoyed getting injured, exactly, I did learn that the fear of getting hurt is by far more debilitating than actually being hurt itself. As Roosevelt said, 'The only thing to fear is fear itself.' Once that fear is gone, what is left is sheer, raw animal aggression. With the will to win, the heart to win and an utter lack of fear, you are going to win. It is as simple as that.

7

THE LADIES OF
THE NIGHT

As I was a trusted bodyguard by now and a person who had shown his mettle on numerous occasions, my friends in East London started to offer me new and challenging work that came with a great deal of responsibility – looking after their women. They had three types of women in their care – their wives and girlfriends, and then the prostitutes who worked in the brothels that they ran, often in return for vast profits, because it is true what they say: it is the oldest profession in the world and the market is always there. Both my associates' girlfriends and prostitutes needed protection, the former from jealous rivals of their men and the latter from aggressive punters, rival pimps and general scumbags who don't understand that working girls are ordinary women with the same rights to protection and physical integrity as anyone else.

One of the people I knew hired me to watch over his girlfriend because she had a stalker and was, understandably, very disturbed to know that an unhinged man was watching her all the time and waiting for his opportunity to do whatever it was he wanted to do to her. One night I was sleeping on the lady's couch in her fancy house when her stalker turned up with a knife and managed to let himself in by popping the double-glazed unit out of the kitchen window and crawling through. He was clearly mad, rolling his eyes and making wild proclamations. I woke up and approached him, telling him to fuck off or take the consequences. He tried to get me with the weapon, but I managed to get the knife from him and chased him out of the flat. I felt that I had earned my money on that contract – although I probably wasn't supposed to have fallen asleep.

Because prostitution is illegal, the women are often reluctant to call on the police whenever anything goes wrong and, even if they do, by then it is usually too late for the police to do anything about it. Furthermore, because of the nature of the business that prostitutes are engaged in, they are often treated without a great deal of sympathy by the police and the general public, many of whom seem to feel that they have got whatever is coming to them. All of that means that private security is hugely important for working girls who know very well how vulnerable they are. Because I worked in a lot of different clubs all over London, I saw every aspect of the sex industry, which is one of Britain's biggest businesses, with customers and sellers from literally every walk of life. Brothels offer a relatively cut-and-dried service where everyone knows what is being bought and sold and, of course, everyone knows where brothels are and how they operate, although they look likely to remain illegal for the foreseeable future.

Some aspects of the sex business were less clear-cut than brothels, however, with lots of grey areas where there was a considerable lack of clarity as to exactly what was being bought and what was being sold. There were clubs with lap dancers and pole dancers where some girls would sell sex and some girls wouldn't, depending on their personal inclinations and how badly they were in debt on that particular week.

These clubs were operating legal businesses, but anything that the girls offered on the side wasn't strictly legit, with management largely turning a blind eye, considering that it was nobody's business but the girls'. This meant that the rules of the game were rather opaque, and that punters could get irate because their mate might have just paid out a hundred quid for a blow job only for them to give the girl in the next booth a hefty wad of notes and get nothing but a bit of a dance in exchange.

Because some of the punters were getting the girls' sexual favours, the ones who weren't were usually very angry to learn that they had just blown half a week's salary on nothing. They would start huffing and puffing and threatening to blow the house down or shouting that they were going to hurt one of the girls. That was when we had to step in and sort things out. We would throw those guys out on their ears. Usually they would leave relatively quietly with just a bit of shouting and cursing. If they were violent, we would bash them up a bit to help them out the door, because there were no statutory rights to a blow job here. That was easy and I didn't lose any sleep over wounding the pride of some loser who thought that handing over half his pay packet meant he had an automatic right to do whatever he wanted with someone else's body.

Then there were the brothels. The way I saw it, the prostitutes were largely victims of their own backgrounds, making a living as best they could with the resources that were available to them. A lot of them had grown up in circumstances very much like my own and had fairly limited educational backgrounds and little by way of a support network, and others had come from abroad in search of a better future only to find that the only way that they could make real money in the United Kingdom was by selling their bodies to the highest bidder. Far from being pathetic and powerless, most of them were perfectly nice, well-balanced girls who any man would have been proud to take home and introduce to his mum. Many of them were mothers with all the concerns that mums usually have, and very unlike the desperate, hollow-eyed junkies of popular imagination. Of all the prostitutes I met, very few had a drug problem. For the vast majority of girls I knew, prostitution was a way of paying the rent and buying school uniforms and putting food on the table.

The girls usually started work around four o'clock in the afternoon and closed by ten, or ten-thirty at the latest, in order to avoid the drunks coming out of the pubs. This is standard procedure. Most of the brothels, then as now, were in quite ordinary flats above shops on ordinary high streets. They had intercom systems to communicate with prospective punters on the street, which gave them a limited degree of control over who they let in. If a prospective customer was obviously drunk, for example, he would be filtered out straight away. Security was always important, because there was always the possibility that someone might turn nasty.

The brothels didn't advertise overtly – no straightforward listings in the Yellow Pages – but everyone knew where they were and there was never any shortage of customers from every walk of life. At the time I was providing security, most of the girls were from Eastern Europe and Russia with the Russian girls particularly popular with the punters because, in fatalistic Russian style, many of them did not insist on using condoms to have sex. This may have been stupid, but it was also a very lucrative line of business. Many, if not most, of the punters on the street operated a head-in-the-sand policy towards AIDS and other sexually transmitted diseases, and they preferred to have sex without a rubber.

When I worked the cheaper brothels, most nights were uneventful in the extreme. We would make sure that the girls didn't get hurt or hassled, have a cup of tea and a bit of a chat with them and then go home. The brothels were small apartments, just about five rooms with a girl in each room, and those girls got to know each other very well, as there was usually plenty of time to chat between jobs. The punters would ring the doorbell downstairs and then, if they were let in, come upstairs and pick a girl.

Most of the customers were regulars who could be trusted to behave reasonably well and pay their bill before leaving, and regulars generally had their own special friends among the girls. I think that some of the friendships were even quite genuine. Even in a relationship in which money changed hands, affection and respect of a sort could flourish on both sides. We, the hired muscle, had to stay out of the way as much as possible when there were customers around so that we wouldn't intimidate the men, but we did get to know the girls well. Most were fine, normal young women just doing their best to make a living and take care of their kids, and I had nothing but respect for them. I will say this: anyone who uses the services of prostitutes while looking down on them and what they do deserves a good hiding.

Although this work was largely quite uneventful, a few incidents stand out as worthy of note. During one period, a gang of African lowlifes (lowlifes came in every nationality; these ones just happened to be Africans) had taken to barging into East End brothels at the end of the night, raping the women, beating them up and taking their money. This had happened on several occasions in a number of different establishments, so everyone was understandably nervous and girls were refusing to go to work without twenty-four-hour protection.

As luck had it, the gang of marauders called by the night I was protecting the girls. Myself and this black guy I knew were waiting at the top of the stairwell when they came thundering upstairs, unaware that we were lying in wait and more than ready to give them what they had coming to them. We had seen them approaching on CCTV, so we were very well prepared. We had to be, as we were seriously outnumbered. When the first guy reached the top of the stairs, I hit him hard in the mouth with a baseball bat and his heavy body fell back down the stairs as he screamed like a pig with a slit throat. Blood and broken teeth poured out of his mouth and down the front of his shirt. He fell on top of his friends who were coming up behind him in the narrow stairwell and they all went down like dominoes, so it was easy for me and my mate to go downstairs and make sure that none of them would want to return in a hurry. We had locked the door remotely so we took the time to do our job well and hurt them as much as they had hurt the women they had beaten. I did not feel sorry for them in the slightest. In my book, rapists deserve whatever they get, and rape is rape, regardless of who the victim happens to be.

Having beaten the intruders soundly, my mate and I had a problem. It was two fold. First of all, because they had all fallen on top of each other in a very narrow stairwell, they were blocking the front door in a big, moaning heap. Secondly, while we had been defending the girls from being robbed and badly hurt, we had also been very enthusiastic in our violence, which meant that when the police arrived we, as well as they, might be in trouble. To avoid difficulties of any kind, we had to go back upstairs, climb out a back window on to a flat roof and shimmy down the drainpipe to make a swift exit.

Most of the time, the work was far less dramatic, but it was certainly interesting, sitting there in the brothel and watching the customers come and go. It was a real lesson in the sociology of the sex industry. The punters came in all ages, shapes and ethnic varieties and did a good job of representing the diversity of London. In the East End, most of them were respectable enough small-business owners, Pakistanis, Indians and Englishmen. The typical punter is the type of guy who sells you your newspaper on your way to work in the morning, and your six-pack of beer when you are on your way home. He is the man who will chat to you about the weather or comment on the football last night or the latest newspaper headlines. He is your neighbour, your teacher, your local shopkeeper. He is just a regular, ordinary man. He might even be you. These fellows came in all tidy in their flannel trousers with their shirts tucked in and then they went upstairs and gave those girls all they had before going back home to have their tea with their wives and children, who presumably remained blissfully ignorant of what Dad got up to on his way home from work.

Most of the ordinary punters just wanted regular, boring missionary-style sex that was over in minutes, but some of the girls had gruesome stories to tell about the less orthodox tastes of some of their clients. I remember one girl having us in stitches as she described a particular client, an Indian shopkeeper who was generally a model of propriety. This dignified and well-dressed gentleman kept the nail on his little finger long, filed and polished and he took his pleasure by coming to the brothel and paying top dollar to insert his precious nail up the girl's bum. Once he got it in, he would wiggle it around so that he could go home with a little collection of, well, poo, under his fingernail. One can only wonder what he did with it when he went home, but that was what he wanted to do, and, if he was prepared to pay for it, that was nobody's business but his own. Excrement is a very popular fetish, I learned. Another punter's only pleasure in life was being shit on, and I almost fell off my chair with laughter when the girl told me, in all earnestness, that she made sure he went home satisfied, by asking him to give her a day's notice so that she could have a big curry the night before he was due to come, because she knew that she would be expected to come up with the goods and she wanted to be prepared. 'I don't want him to go home disappointed, Paul. He's one of my best customers!'

Yes, excrement featured quite frequently in some of the girls' more lurid tales. Well, it takes all sorts.

So much for the East End brothels. I thought that I had seen everything after a stint working in them. But then I got put on security detail in the West End, and realised that I hadn't had a clue about what real perversion entails! If you want to learn about perversion, you have got to spend some time with the upper classes because – take it from me – they are the experts.

In the West End, the brothel clients were mainly Members of Parliament, minor members of the royal family, aristocrats, senior civil servants and businessmen. They were all very well-heeled and they came with thick wallets, credit cards and serious psychological issues that expressed themselves in the form of unorthodox sexual preferences. You see, the fees in this much more upper-crust establishment were very high, and the business only catered to the top end of the market. The girls, however, were not notably different from their East End colleagues – they just had fewer tattoos, more confidence and middle-class accents. A greater number of them had Oxbridge degrees, and very few of them had drug or other substance problems.

The punters, however, were a great deal more interesting than in the East End and the need for security was even more stringent. Various factors were at play. On the one hand, because these girls were so expensive – we are talking about between five hundred and a thousand pounds a go, quite a few years ago – there was the risk that some punters would try to leave without paying for their hour or two of fun. On the other hand, some of the punters were so well known and so easily recognised that security had to be discreet as they certainly did not want to have their extra-marital exploits splashed all over the tabloids. Also, the level of perversion and extreme sex play that was requested was extraordinary and it seemed that the more blue the blood that ran in the customer's veins, the weirder the tastes that needed to be catered to. When you saw a guy going in with a bowler hat and a copy of the *Financial Times*, you just knew that he was going to ask to be dressed in a nappy, or something equally undignified.

Because I was an outsider in this well-connected world, I was not privy to the unspoken rules of the community, and the situation made me feel a bit uneasy, because, when you don't know the rules, it is easy to put a foot wrong by mistake. It was much simpler in the East End where, if someone started to cause a problem, I just beat them up, got the money they owed from them and threw them out to lick their wounds and slink away. I was familiar with life on the streets of the East End because that was the environment in which I had grown up, come of age and acquired all my work experience. There I could read the body language, interpret the nuances and know when and how to go in for the blow. There, I not only knew the unspoken rules, but I was an expert on them. Here I couldn't do that, because the offender in question might well be minor royalty, or an important magistrate, or a visiting dignitary from overseas. While we had had to be reasonably discreet in the East End, here we had to hide from the customers completely and keep up the pretence that there was no security at all, even though security was at least as important here as in the grottier end of the market.

The security detail had a special room with cameras observing who went in and out of the lavishly appointed quarters – although not what happened in the bedrooms, of course – and a full sound system so that we could hear what was happening everywhere and make sure that only the people who got hurt actually *wanted* to be hurt and that the prostitutes didn't have to do anything that they hadn't agreed to. There were the guys who liked to tie girls up and play bondage games with them, pretending to dominate the prostitute or take her by force. There was always one who would go a bit too far with his game, and when the girl started to say, 'No, no, no, I don't want this any more,' we would have to go in and put a stop to it before she got hurt.

All the girls' rooms were fitted with panic buttons: on the bed, on the mattress where they could be activated by hitting the bed three times, and on all the furniture around the room so that, whatever the customer asked the girl to do, she was always able to reach a panic button whenever she felt that the situation was getting out of hand. There were also recognised code words that, when the girls uttered them, would have us out of our room and into the girl's in a matter of moments. There were often times when someone was causing a problem but we couldn't beat him up and throw him out because he was too important and it would be more than our job was worth. We would have to call him 'sir' as we gently but firmly escorted him to the door and helped him to pull up his trousers before sending him on his way. While the temptation was always to get a bit rough with them if they caused difficulties, we had to handle these idiots with kid gloves and treat them with respect regardless of how stupidly they had been behaving inside.

The best thing about working in the posh brothels in the West End was the light relief, and there was certainly plenty of that, thanks to the state-of-the-art sound system and customers who literally seemed to have no shame. There were many times when I and the other security guys had to stuff our fists into our mouths to stop our laughter from being heard as we sat in our secret chamber listening to the extraordinary antics of our social 'superiors'. It was a real eye-opener.

Because these girls were earning such shitloads of money, most of them were expected, and prepared, to do a lot of very strange stuff in return. There were the usual common or garden variety perversions: financiers who liked to dress up as babies and get smacked for dirtying their giant nappies or high court judges who wanted the girl to dress up like the matron in the public schools that they had attended years before. There were a surprising number of lawyers, Members of Parliament and Harley Street doctors who wanted nothing more than to be shagged by women with massive strap-on dildos that looked as though they had been designed to hurt. The more educated the client, the kinkier; that was the general rule. Those with higher degrees from Oxford and Cambridge seemed to enjoy cutting off their air supplies to maximise their climax. Perhaps it was all those years they had spent in science class that made them come up with such manoeuvres – or could it be all the free time they had on their hands? Every second ex-public school boy wanted to call his prostitute 'Mummy' which makes you wonder how damaged they were by their version of being abandoned by their parents to be raised in an institution, no matter how lavish and well appointed.

A lot of what went on between the punters and the prostitutes seemed to be only secondarily about sex and more about control and power or, more importantly, the ceding of control and power to someone else. These were important men with a lot of responsibility in their lives and I suppose that perhaps they wanted not to have to be in charge for a change. We are talking about the men who decide the laws by which we are all supposed to live, who decide who goes to prison and who goes free, and who hold the destiny of the United Kingdom, in a very real sense, in their hands. That responsibility must have weighed heavily on their shoulders at times, and shooting their load was how they lightened their burden.

I remember one very important, very wealthy man in his fifties who would regularly hire three or four expensive girls to strap on massive dildos and fuck him up the arse while he cried out for more. This would literally go on for hours until he must have been bleeding from both ends. We security guards would all wonder how on earth he managed to have a crap after having had such a going-over. It would all start off quite funny, but by the end you couldn't help but wince at the thought of what the gentleman was putting his body through. It was hard work for the prostitutes, too, and they certainly felt that they had earned their money after a session with him. The girls would have to pause every so often to rest and catch their breath and he would shout, in his plummy accent, 'Don't you dare fucking stop! Don't you dare fucking stop! I'm paying you good money for this! Give it to me good! Come on, Mummy. Who's been a naughty boy then?'

This guy was one of our favourites. We used to

laugh our heads off whenever he came around. I wish that I could name names, but I can't so you'll just have to imagine who it was. Aim high, and you won't be far wrong.

The girls despised some of their customers, often with good reason, but there were others who were regular visitors to the establishment of whom they grew genuinely fond – a bunch of well-heeled elderly gents who gave them a lot of money and mostly wanted to talk to them rather than get up to anything saucy, either because they were just too old to have sex, or because they were simply desperately lonely and wanted the companionship of a pretty young woman for an hour or two. They might get jerked off, but then they would want to sit and talk about their lives or their current obsessions. In exchange for listening to these lonely old men, and sometimes for going out with them to a bar or restaurant, the girls received very large sums of money and felt fortunate in doing so.

While the East End brothels might have feared being closed down by the cops, the West End ones had no such fears, as the police were regular visitors, albeit not in any professional capacity. They were either getting backhanders or free sessions with the girls. Either way, they came out looking very happy with life in general.

Prostitutes and punters are both victims of stereotyping. Not all the girls are desperate and sad and not all the men are victimisers. I have worked for too long in some of the strangest places to think that it is always easy to pigeonhole people. Take it from me; it isn't. I have met some serious people who were real gentlemen, and some supposed gentlemen who would kill your grandmother and sell her if they thought there was a market for dead grannies. Nothing is ever as simple as it seems, and life is not painted in black and white but in multiple shades of grey.

I have been asked if it was depressing working for the brothels, and I can see where the question is coming from. I am not blinkered. I know that there are some girls for whom prostitution can become a trap from which it is difficult to escape. All I can say now, looking back many years later, is that I didn't find it depressing at the time because I felt that protecting the girls was a job that somebody had to do, and that it might as well be me as anybody else, especially because I knew that I had the means, the ability and the willingness to do whatever it took to make sure that nothing bad happened to them. The way I saw it, the girls were in a very vulnerable situation, and they were much better off protected than not. Most of the girls were going to be prostitutes anyway, so the alternative to their working in a protected environment was taking to the streets, where any lowlife drug addict could and probably would have had a go at them.

For me, at the time when I was doing the work, it offered good money and great insight into human nature, and it was a way to keep the money flowing while I continued studying and working hard to become a personal trainer. It gave me the time I needed to work out in the gym and to study, and I was glad for the opportunity. Would I do it now? Well, no. But then I am not the person now that I was then. In those days, the work enabled me to get the proper education that I had never received as a child and adolescent and for that, if nothing else, I was grateful to have it.

I was also glad that I had put St Leonard's almost completely behind me, and I was proud of how much I had achieved in the gym despite or perhaps even because of the injuries that I had suffered when I fell off the roof. While I accepted with bitter regret the fact that I would never be a professional boxer, there was no way I was going to let what had happened to me stand in the way of my goal of doing the sort of work I knew that I was best at. A lot of my colleagues in the gym and on the doors were on steroids and other illegal substances that helped to keep them bulked up, but I was built and buff thanks to my own tireless efforts, and I was thinking increasingly of a future in which I wouldn't have to work for anyone but could be my own boss instead. Quite a few of the men I worked with back then are now dead as a result of their steroid abuse, so, once again, I am deeply thankful that I was never tempted to take drugs of any kind, and I know that the rigorous training I had received in the boxing club had given me the discipline I needed. The physiology courses I had to take as I studied to become a personal trainer also showed me, in graphic detail, what steroid abuse would do to my insides.

Although I was earning very good money, I did not want to be the hired muscle indefinitely. That was why I was working and studying so hard to acquire all the qualifications I would need to work in some of the best gyms in the country. It was time to move on from all that – and things were just beginning to take off in the more normal circles into which I was gradually moving.

8

PERSONAL TRAINER TO THE STARS

I got lucky when I was offered a job in the Barbican in the City as a free-weights manager. I knew that, if I worked hard and gave the job all I had, this could be a seriously good break for me. The gym in the Barbican was one of the best in the business, and it deserved its stellar reputation because it provided a top service at one of the best locations in London.

Having successfully completed a series of professional courses, which I had funded in full on my own from the money I made providing security to brothels and working on the doors, I had started doing personal training seriously. Initially, I was still on security detail and doing a little mini-cab driving to pay the rent. The late 1980s was a time when personal trainers were almost unheard of and, in fact, I was one of the very first in the country and often had to sit down and explain exactly what I did to prospective clients who had never heard of the profession. Little by little, as a result of hard graft and being in the right place at the right time, the personal training became the most important element of my career. I got the Barbican gig out of sheer luck, and it certainly helped to launch my new venture. About thirty people had applied for the role, and I just happened to be the one to get the job. I don't know why they liked me best, but I am certainly very glad that they did.

The Barbican was definitely the best place for me to be at this point in my life, and it opened a lot of doors for me, both professionally and socially. It also helped with my self-esteem; they would not have hired me if they had thought I was the sort of person Auntie Coral had insisted I would become, would they? Because the Barbican was a top-class gym, it had a lot of very wealthy members from the professional classes and the world of show business, and it was also the gym of choice for many of the world's celebrities from stage and screen when they were in town for one reason or another. The employees of the gym had to know how to look casual when the likes of Christopher Reeve (Superman!), Jodie Foster, our own Charles Dance, Janet Street-Porter and other celebrities, foreign and home-grown, came in. The regular customers, most of whom were company directors, wealthy lawyers and the like, also tried to look unimpressed as they nonchalantly got on with their own fitness regimes. Of course, they usually failed.

It would be nice to be able to tell you that I became close personal friends with a lot of my celebrity clients but, while most of them were perfectly cordial and polite whenever I interacted with them, I was one of the help and a personal relationship of any sort wasn't really on the cards. And, in fact, because of all the non-disclosure agreements that I was asked to sign whenever I worked with someone famous enough to warrant one, I can't tell you very much about it at all. Suffice to say that I often had to pinch myself to make sure that this was really happening; that this was really me, Paul Connolly, the runt from St Leonard's children's home, working with the men and women most people only see on TV or when they go to the cinema.

Because I had a strong background in boxing, boxing training and elements of the sport were an integral part of what I did. Those unfamiliar with the art of boxing usually don't realise that training to become a boxer isn't just about throwing punches and being tough, but is a subtle and complex affair that calls for working on the body's strength, agility and musculature with a great deal of understanding of anatomy and physiology. Really good boxers know a lot about how their bodies work and, even when they are not very highly educated in an academic sense, they are always very knowledgeable in every practical way that matters to the professional athlete.

Thanks to my studies, I was now able to approach the subject of personal training from the viewpoint of a boxer and a fitness trainer. Customers were curious about boxing, so most of my clients wanted to do work that integrated elements from that sport with what they already knew from aerobics. I already knew from my own experience that boxing training is the best all-over workout you can get because boxers are not just strong and able to channel aggression but also extremely fit. I quickly realised that elements of boxing training can easily be adapted to the needs of anyone who wants to get fit, from the daintiest young woman to the bulkiest doorman. The clients loved my workouts and enjoyed the elements of boxing that I worked into them, and I started to become quite well known on the fitness circuit at a time when boxing was still, for almost everyone, just for boxers. Word spread about the services I had on offer, and I was often asked, 'Can I do a bit of one-to-one boxing with you, then?' Life is strange. I had planned to become a professional boxer, been thwarted in my plans and now I found myself boxing again. In an odd way, my dream had come true, albeit not exactly as I had imagined it as a young kid in the ring at Dagenham Boxing Club.

Becoming sought after meant that I had to learn how to talk to famous people without appearing star-struck or overly impressed. The last thing the celebrity clients of upmarket clubs want is to have to deal with people fawning all over them, and they are entitled to work out without having to worry about being treated differently to anyone else.

Nowadays, integrating some boxing training into a workout is old news, but at the time we were the first ones doing it in Britain. We were doing it long before it became hip. We made it hip, in fact. I developed a series of exercises and workouts that was unique to me and started to sell my services all over London to an increasingly eager clientele. I showed my clients how to strap and tape their hands up like real boxers, how to make sure that they were warmed up properly and that their technique was good, and how to cool down and stretch out – all the basic skills that I had learned in the course of my many years in the boxing ring. I combined everything that I knew from my boxing training with the scientific knowledge I had acquired from the studies I had done in working towards becoming a personal trainer.

My style wasn't that of a traditional boxing coach. Boxing coaches come from the old school and do ballistics stretches and other exercises that can be unsafe for regular clients who don't have the strength or fitness to deal with them. I was teaching boxing to the general public, so I had to know how to look after them properly. Not being athletes, most people can't be trained like boxers. Continuing with my work, I developed a system of exercise called Boxerobics™ and started my classes at Dance Works on Oxford Street, another gym with a top-notch clientele. I was proud of what I was doing, because I felt that my work was not just providing me with a living, but also making a positive difference in the lives of the people who signed up to use me as their trainer. I could see for myself how they felt better physically and better about themselves psychologically as they became more fit, stronger and healthier.

Things were going very well, but I still had to do a little door work in the evenings to pay the bills. Then something fantastic happened. The media started to notice me.

Because of the high profile of the gyms where I was working, not to mention of the celebrity clients and media types who frequented those gyms, and the growing popularity of boxing training as a keep-fit method, *Time Out* did a magazine piece on me, and *Health and Fitness* magazine started to do a weekly segment on me too. Other health and leisure publications quickly followed suit. At the time, I was the only personal trainer in London doing boxing, Boxerobics™ and boxing training. In fact, I was one of the very few personal trainers in

London at all, as this was a profession that was then in its infancy. While some trainers were offering boxing exercises without knowing anything about boxing, and some boxing coaches were opening classes to the general public with no awareness of what ordinary health-club members can achieve and what is too dangerous for them to attempt, I was able to straddle both worlds. I discovered that I was a very good communicator, and much more articulate than I had previously thought. It didn't seem to matter that I had dropped out of school young; I was still more than able to get my ideas across in a way that my clients could understand and appreciate.

As I was becoming well known and acquiring a healthy reputation in London and around the country, I attracted the attention of a company called Pickwick Pictures that was planning to make a fitness video with a beautiful Australian super-model named Elle MacPherson, who went by the moniker 'The Body' because, it was said, she had the most perfect physique of any woman in the world. I was approached by Pickwick Pictures while I was working in the Barbican.

'We want to make a video called *The Body Workout*, with Elle MacPherson,' they explained, 'and we need to have some boxing in it. We've heard that you are the man for boxing. Would you be interested in working on the pilot for the video?'

Even I had heard of Elle MacPherson but I tried to look unimpressed as though I worked with celebrities of her calibre all the time.

'Perhaps. I'm quite busy. I'll have to check my schedule.'

'OK. Look, we'll do some work in London and then we'll fly you over to America and we'll see how we get on. Does that sound good to you?'

'Well, like I said, I'll have to check my schedule,' I answered, although inside I was rejoicing.

Wow. Was this really me? Paul Connolly from St Leonard's children's home? Was the loser, the reject, the kid whom nobody had ever loved or wanted, really being asked if he would like to work with a world-famous supermodel?

As I said, I had been approached by Pickwick Pictures because boxing had suddenly become hugely popular, but very few trainers knew how to apply boxing techniques to the prospective buyers of the video that Elle MacPherson was planning to make. I was one of the very few in the world and at that time probably the only suitable fitness expert in the United Kingdom. They needed someone who would be able to tailor-make a fitness programme for the general public that could be done at home with no supervision and no risk to anyone's health and well-being. This was quite a demanding challenge, as the exercises that boxers have to do can cause a great deal of strain to ordinary bodies.

The pilots that I made were shown to Elle. She liked them and they were duly used in shooting *The Body Workout* video. After we had worked in London for quite a while, once they were completely happy with the product, they flew me out to Miami to make the pilot video proper. Until then I had not travelled very widely, and Miami was a tremendously exciting place for me to visit. Of all the cities in the United States, it is the most 'Latin', with vibrant colours and smells and sounds unlike anything I had seen or heard before.

As the pilot had gone so well, it was decided that the video would be made and marketed. *The Body Workout* was shot in New Zealand with Karen Voight, who is a very well-known trainer in America. I was supposed to be credited as the boxing expert on the video, but, when it eventually came out, my name wasn't on the box or the credits; I watched them a few times just to make sure. This makes me wish that I had had the business knowhow in those days to realise that I needed an agent who would have taken care of my rights and career.

Still, I have all the paperwork and my involvement with *The Body Workout* video launched my career on this side of the Atlantic. I had a connection with a serious video production company and with one of the most famous supermodels on the scene. Astonishingly quickly, people seemed to know who I was and to want to know what I did. A series of newspaper and magazine articles about me and my services followed. I was invited on daytime television regularly, and my career really seemed to be taking off in a big way. The networking opportunities, as they say, were phenomenal. Today, *The Body Workout* is still one of the top-selling exercise videos of all time and I am very proud of my role in the making of it. It was a thrill to see myself featured in the *Sun*'s fitness section, *Bodyworks*, on 26 July 1994. The article went into my involvement with Elle and Pickwick Pictures in some detail:

Elle MacPherson may have the world's most amazing body... but keeping it in shape doesn't come easy.

So the 30-year-old supermodel, dubbed The Body, turned to British fitness expert Paul Connolly and his new boxing workout.

Aussie Elle had piled on the pounds for her role in the sizzling new movie, Sirens, *but when filming finished, she needed to tone up fast for her next project, a new health and fitness video.*

Paul flew out to Miami where her video was being shot to show her the ropes with his new Boxerobics workout.

Paul Connolly pulls no punches when it comes to exercise. The former boxer and fitness instructor is creator of Boxerobics, the variation of the punchy US craze Boxercize that is fast catching on across the UK. A challenging combination of boxing moves and aerobic exercises, Boxercize originally caught the fitness world's attention after actresses including Michelle Pfeiffer and Cher used it to tone up for film roles.

When Health and Fitness first reported the arrival of Boxercize in the UK it was an unsafe workout, often taught by boxers or fitness instructors with little knowledge of each other's profession. This was where Connolly's credentials gave him a head start. He switched from boxing to a career in fitness when an accident meant he had to give up hopes of turning professional.

The *Sun* was perhaps the most widely read of all the articles about me and my work, but it was just one among many. Success breeds success, and the more I was featured in newspapers and magazines, the more the journalists seemed to want to know. In *Time Out* in January 1994, I received a typical, enthusiastic response to what I had to offer. The article said, in part:

Former boxing champion Paul Connolly, who teaches his own rigorous system of 'Boxerobics' at Danceworks in London says that [great results] are accessible to anyone – so long as they do not have specific health problems and are prepared to train sufficiently hard. Boxing, combined with vigorous circuit training, is rivalled only by squash in providing the most comprehensive total-body workout. And it is particularly good for women, since speed and agility of movement prevent muscles from getting bulky...

Over and above such body-shaping benefits, the women I talked to in Connolly's class – which is made up equally of both sexes – valued the cathartic effects of discharging pent-up anger and aggression by punching, hissing and shouting. Fatigue dissolves in minutes, they say, and is replaced by a long-lasting adrenaline 'high'. Confidence grows too, as one's skill and coordination improve.

I tried to stay nonchalant about the attention I was getting, because I knew that I had worked hard for it and that nothing lasts forever and that I would have to continue to work hard if I wanted things to keep going well.

But I did wonder, sometimes, if any of the people from the life that I had left behind me long before had come across the articles about me. Did Bill Starling read the *Sun*? Did Auntie Coral? They might well have done. Would they have recognised the man in the photographs as the miserable, underweight child whose life they had made so very unhappy? And, if they had, would they have cared? I didn't know the answers to these questions, but they continued to come to me, unbidden. And what about my parents? I had no contact with either of them, but somewhere they were continuing to live their lives. Did they know that I was doing OK, despite them? Did they care?

9
FLYING HIGH

I must have inherited the Irish gift of the gab because the important people I was meeting now all seemed to like me, and to want to hear what I had to say, particularly my views on and input into the world of fitness. It felt good to be listened to with respect and to know that I warranted that respect, although there were often times when I didn't feel entirely comfortable with my new surroundings.

Now that I was a known quantity with a product and a service that was fashionable, and that cutting-edge people wanted to buy, important, educated people started approaching me with requests that I write articles for boxing workouts that they were preparing for this or that magazine. It was wonderful, especially for someone like me who had spent years of his life feeling and sometimes even behaving like the sort of person most decent individuals will cross the road to avoid. At times it seemed surreal to think of myself writing for magazines and other publications that thousands of people would read, when just a few years earlier I had had to submit myself to the embarrassment of an adult literacy course, because I couldn't even read well enough to make my way through a tabloid newspaper or figure out the signs in shop windows. I had to use spellcheckers a lot but the excitement of being able to express myself clearly in written English never wore off.

I was approached by *Cosmopolitan* magazine, probably the most influential of all the women's magazines on the market at the time. The health and fitness editors at that time were two women, Mary Coomer and Eve Cameron, who wanted to know if I would write a regular column for their readers, and I was delighted to have the opportunity to reach a wider audience through the pages of their magazine.

Boxerobics™ was suitable for clients of both sexes, but women in particular seemed to enjoy it, probably in part because it gives them the means to work some aggression out of their systems, which is something that a lot of females appreciate, having less opportunity than men to be aggressive in their daily lives. The *Cosmo* editors liked the work that I did for them and the response from the readers was very positive.

Then Mary rang me up. 'Get yourself a passport,' she said, 'because we need you to start travelling with us.'

I had never travelled very much until then, and, although I was an adult, I was as wide-eyed and excited as a child to arrive in San Francisco and see the Golden Gate Bridge and all the sights. There I worked at an upmarket private health and athletics club in Silicon Valley. Silicon Valley was booming at the time, and there was money everywhere and lots of very well-heeled computer aficionados (or 'geeks', as I call them) who wanted to look buff despite their desk jobs.

I was amazed by the difference in attitude between London and San Francisco, in particular among the people working in the world of fitness, which is a competitive arena with a lot of egos involved. Back home, if I said, 'I worked on the pilot for Elle MacPherson's video,' other trainers would shuffle away muttering, 'Who the fuck does he think he is? Thinks he's better than the rest of us, does he?' and I would be left feeling as though I had been showing off unnecessarily. I don't like that about the United Kingdom. One person's success is seen to diminish the other people he knows. In America, it was different. Will Willis, one of the guys I worked with – a former Mr U.S.A. and therefore no slouch himself – saw my CV one day. 'High five, buddy!' Will said. 'Elle MacPherson. Right on!'

In America, people like to be around success, so, if you are successful and you are their friend, they feel that some of it rubs off on them. In Britain, they just don't want you getting too uppity.

I continued to travel quite widely for a time, and I believe that this was the best education I ever had, because it opened my eyes in a way nothing ever had before. I saw vast swathes of America. I saw the Caribbean. I saw most of Europe.

Experiencing other cultures, other people and other ways of doing things showed me how tiny and insignificant my part of the world was by comparison. This in turn made me realise that the people, places and things that had always intimidated me were not actually that scary at all. Who cared, outside East London, who was in and who wasn't? Who cared who was able to take on whom and come out the best? Who cared where I had grown up? Outside Britain, nobody knew that I had grown up in a children's home. Nobody knew that I had been thrown out with the rubbish as a baby or that nobody had ever wanted me. Also, outside the United Kingdom, few if any people could tell from my accent and the way I talked, walked and behaved that I was anything other than an educated, sophisticated individual like themselves. In fact, I was now good friends with people from all walks of life and all parts of the world – bankers, technology professionals and architects. If they didn't look down on me, why should anyone, and why should I?

My life had gone crazy as I was launched into a glamorous world where I often felt I didn't belong, although nobody else seemed to share that view. Following my success in the print media, I was contacted by a television production company to see if I would be interested in making some live appearances on television. Of course I would! Soon I was on Channel Four's *Big Breakfast* show with Paula Yates every morning as fitness expert of the week. *The Big Breakfast* was enormous in those days, so this was a major coup for me. I had the experience of working with Paula out in front of the cameras and got to know her a little by spending time chatting with her both before and after my appearances. Paula was a lovely, sexy woman who was a lot of fun and not vain or standoffish in the slightest, but completely approachable and down-to-earth. Unlike a lot of television 'personalities' who think that being in the public eye means that the sun shines out of their arse, Paula had no vanity about her, but instead treated everyone the same.

Paula used to come in to work at five or six in the morning with her bleached platinum-blonde hair on end and bags under her eyes, looking as though she had been up clubbing all night – which, knowing Paula, was more than likely. Five minutes later, hair and make-up done, she was looking spunky and beautiful and ready for the cameras and whatever the day was going to throw at her. She was a natural in show business; her energy lit up the screen. Paula knew that I was nervous, so, to put me at ease, she flirted with me and pinched my bum until I was laughing too much to worry about what was going on. I had been anxious about doing live TV in the beginning, but Paula got me to relax with her high jinks and soon I felt very much at home under the bright lights of the television studio.

I met Pierce Brosnan, Julie Walters, Robin Williams and Michael Hutchence. But much more than any of them, I was bowled over by the puppet duo Zig and Zag. Zig and Zag, the brainchildren of a couple of Irish blokes, were hugely popular at the time, and it was hilarious watching the filming and seeing both the characters come to life and the puppeteers, lying on the floor out of view of the cameras. Having said that, Julie Walters was lovely too and I certainly don't mean to put her in second place to a pair of puppets. We chatted in the Green Room for ages, and she was so far from putting on airs and graces that I didn't even realise who I was talking to until later! Pierce Brosnan and Robin Williams were extremely personable and friendly in the brief time that we spent together.

I also worked with presenter Gaby Roslyn, but

she was a lot more reserved than Paula, Chris Evans or any of the superstars, to put it mildly. The impression one got from the established stars was that they felt no need to be standoffish, because they were good at what they did, and very comfortable in their own skins.

Featuring on *The Big Breakfast* turned me into a recognisable face and a sellable proposition. Media types are lazy, so, if someone has been on one show and gone down well, they're more likely to invite them on to the next show rather than look for someone else. This was good for me. The next thing I knew, I was on all the morning shows because all of a sudden everyone wanted a piece of the boxing mania. From initially feeling quite overwhelmed about the whole thing, I started to feel that I was operating in an environment in which I belonged. I featured on *Under the Moon* on Channel Four with Nigel Benn, a middleweight boxing champion, and Tom Binns, a sports presenter. I had to take my Boxerobics class, composed of men and women, into the studio and do a class for them. *Under the Moon* was a lads' show, all boobs and sport with cheerleaders and sportsmen.

I was also invited to feature as an interviewee on *The Word*, a Friday-night show with Dani Behr, but that was a bit of a disappointment, as I should have realised from the show's target demographic of late-night drunks. I thought that I was going to be given a serious interview, but, when I got to the studio, I was asked to strip down to the waist, run on to the set, pick up Dani and run off the set with her. In the end, I never made the cut because the show ran out of time. What a waste of energy!

I had to go to Birmingham to feature on the *Anne and Nick Show*. We had a boxing ring set up, and some of the girls I was working with did a boxing routine for the cameras – I also chatted with Jeremy Beadle who was another really nice bloke. A while after that, I was on the *Ross King Show* featuring Boxerobics™ for the BBC.

I occasionally wondered if anyone from my old life had seen me on television, but I never tried to find out for sure.

Flushed with success, I applied for a trademark for Boxerobics™ and set up a company that ran courses in the London boxing gyms aimed at the city trainers who would each pay me a hundred pounds a day to do a course. Using boxing techniques as part of an everyday fitness routine was the latest best thing and all the trainers wanted a piece of the action. Luckily for me, I was one of the very few people around with the proper qualifications to teach them what they needed to know. Suddenly, at a time when most trainers were getting twenty pounds a class, I was making a hundred and twenty and bringing in five or six grand a week. It was like a dream come true.

Another dividend of this success was that being on television and in so many magazines and newspapers meant that I could sleep with pretty much any woman who caught my eye, and usually did. I remember one girl who always wanted to have sex with me in the gym just before the rest of the class arrived, because she liked the thrill of nearly getting caught and was turned on by the characteristic smell of the rubber floor mats. I wasn't going to argue; if that was her dream, who was I to stand in her way?

There were times when I would wake up in the morning and wonder if this was really me, the little shit from St Leonard's whom nobody had ever loved. Had Starling or Coral seen me on television and wished that they had been a little bit nicer? The bastards!

If I'd had an agent back then, I am sure he could have kept the ball rolling. I am the first to admit that I had very little in the way of business know-how. Boxing as part of an everyday fitness routine continued to be popular, and I soon acquired competitors. Still, I made enough money to buy my first house, in cash. Getting the keys to my own home was a very important moment for me and it was wonderful to know that I had shown myself and the world that I could stand on my own two feet and make a success of myself.

I almost ran into trouble when one of the

newspapers ran a story about me and one of the celebrities I worked for, implying that there was more going on between us than met the eye. The implication in the article that we had, in fact, slept together was very clear. Of course, nothing of the sort had happened, but the woman's boyfriend was furious and my good relationship with my client suffered badly as, despite all my protestations to the contrary, there remained the lingering suspicion that I had made false claims. I was furious. The newspaper had to print a retraction and, although I had neither slept with the woman nor suggested that anything untoward had happened between us, I ended up losing that particular job. I have been very wary of journalists ever since, having seen for myself how words can be twisted to mean something completely different.

At this point in my life, I was happier, more relaxed and calmer than ever before, and I had even begun to respect myself a little, and not just because of my ability to hurt people with my fists, but because I was now able to use my skills and knowledge to help clients make their lives better.

But the old demons that had been haunting me all my life had not gone away completely; not at all. Now that I was making a good living doing what I loved, I no longer had to do very much door work, but I kept my hand in for when personal training work was slow and, even more, because I still enjoyed the opportunity to drop the people who deserved it and see them limp away, bruised and suitably chastened. A part of me needed to know that, when I felt the need to hurt someone, I would have both the opportunity and the means to give it to the sort of bloke who had it coming to him. Working on the doors gave me plenty of chances to vent the pent-up rage that I had never managed to purge, and I was reluctant to turn my back completely on those opportunities.

Now that I was moving in wider circles and also feeling more confident about myself, I started to make more friends outside the world of door work and the gym, including my mate, Ian, who I met when he was putting the computer system into a gym where I was working as a manager. Ian, who had also grown up in Essex, lived just around the corner from my new house, and, although we were very different in many ways, we soon became good friends. Neither of us had a wife and family at the time so we started enjoying the bachelor life together.

Having caught the travel bug through work, I now wanted to do more of it, and to do it on my own account. In 1996, Ian and I decided to go to Florida together for a break. Ian had a gold card with Virgin Airlines, so we had breakfast and a massage in the Upper Class Lounge. I was impressed by how all I had to do was look up the right way and a pretty girl came running with a delicious meal; this was a million miles from where I had grown up!

'I could get used to this,' I commented to Ian.

After the meal, we boarded the plane and started to relax into the idea of a couple of well-earned weeks off in the sun.

Just before we were due to take off, two South Londoners got on the plane. One was a huge, well-built man with long, blond hair and the other was a short, stocky guy with cropped hair. They both had idiotic expressions and seemed to be more than a few sandwiches short of a picnic. In short, they looked like trouble. They were. Ian knew me well, so he made sure that I sat on the inside seat, as far away from them as possible, using himself as a buffer.

These two morons started to behave like the dickheads they were as soon as they got on board, to the consternation of all the families on the way to Disneyworld sitting in their vicinity, who now contemplated the horror of having to spend the next eight or so hours in their company. Anyone with eyes in their head could see that they were trouble. Already stinking drunk, the men opened up the overhead compartment, took out Ian's computer bags and threw them into the aisle so that there would be room for their own stuff. Ian didn't say anything. He got out of his seat and quietly rearranged his things. We all looked at the cabin staff with the expectation that they would arrange to have the troublemakers removed before the plane took off, but nothing happened. The senior staff were distracted because they had some trainee hostesses on the flight. Undisturbed, the two geezers got into their seats and remained relatively well behaved during take-off but as soon as the plane was in the air they set about getting even drunker than they already were, which is saying quite a lot. And the drunker they got, the more obnoxious they became. Sitting in the middle of the plane, across from them, I started to fidget. I had to sit on my hands to stop myself from taking action. I was in a closed environment and couldn't stand being around these idiots without doing anything about them. If anyone was asking for a hiding, they were. I had come across their sort – vain, bulked-up bullies with a lot more attitude than brain cells – a thousand times before, but I had usually been in a situation to do something about it. Now I hated not being able to give them what they had coming to them.

Ian looked at me. He knew how tense I was getting and what a temper I had.

'Paul, mate,' he said quietly. 'Please don't do anything you would regret. We're off on our holidays. We're supposed to be having a good time. Don't let those idiots destroy it. They are not worth it. Just ignore them. Just relax!'

'But those pricks threw your bags into the aisle!

They took out your stuff and threw it about so that they could stow their own things away!"

'Yeah, and I'm not doing anything about it, am I? So why should you?'

'Yeah, well…'

'Paul. Please.'

I now literally had to sit on my hands to stop myself from throttling them. But I kept getting angrier and angrier as these two lowlifes kept calling the hostesses to bring them more and more free wine. Presumably because they were inexperienced or just intimidated by them, the hostesses continued to oblige and the booze kept on flowing. Their voices got louder and they started passing remarks about and intimidating the families sitting around them.

Then they noticed me.

I was working out a lot at the time and weighed about thirteen or fourteen stone of pure muscle, which is a lot for a man of my build. I was still doing door work in those days and I needed to be big in order to move people out of clubs and on to the street when they caused trouble. They seemed to feel threatened by my appearance, or at least to feel some sort of a primitive need to establish themselves as the alpha males in this scenario.

One of the drunken idiots caught my eye. I glared at him, and then looked away. I knew that Ian was right. We were in a metal tube at 35,000 feet and they were not worth getting angry about.

I tried to ignore them. But the blond nudged his friend with a sneer all over his stupid mug.

'Look at the dick with the T-shirt and the muscles,' he said in a voice made deliberately loud enough for me to hear. 'He thinks he's so fucking great, don't he? Let's cut him. See if he thinks he's so great then, eh?'

His companion snorted in hilarity.

One of the children sitting in the area started to cry. She had not signed up for this when she had persuaded Mum and Dad to take her to Disneyland.

'Don't. Do. Anything,' Ian instructed me through gritted teeth. 'Just ignore them. It's not worth getting in any trouble over people like that.'

We called a hostess and asked to be moved, but we were told that there were no seats for us to move to and that we would just have to stay put.

The bozos continued calling for more wine, which the hostesses duly provided, and proceeded to go about getting drunker and drunker. About four hours into the flight, they decided that it would be clever to start throwing ice cubes at my head. Now they were fucking asking for it. I had been doing my best, but I had my limits and they had already been exceeded several times over.

I turned to the two idiots and said in the most controlled voice I could muster, 'Do I look like some kind of cunt?'

'You fucking do,' the long-haired one said.

'Because that's what you are and if you want to do something about it you can come over here and I'll cut your fucking throat for you.' He laughed and wiped the wine that was dribbling down his chin with the back of his hand.

Well, that was it. I wasn't going to take any more. I had done my best to stay calm, as Ian advised, but by now they had pushed all my buttons. I jumped right over Ian and headed towards them, and the long-haired guy tried to get up so as to be able to tackle me. In his drunkenness, he swayed slightly. A few of the women sitting in the area started to scream in genuine fear that something awful was going to go wrong.

Before he could get to his feet, I hit him as hard as I could, packing my fourteen stone of muscle into the punch. His head whipped around, and the back of his ear ripped open against the velour of the aeroplane seat. Blood flowed everywhere and he screamed like a little girl in a combination of fear, rage and disbelief that I had dared to take him up on his threats. Then his short-haired pal tried to get up, but he didn't stand a chance. I was angry now and, when I get angry, I can really channel it. I get into the zone and nothing seems to matter except making sure that justice is done. Before the second man could as much as get out into the aisle, I hit him five times – bang, bang, bang, bang, bang – and knocked him back into his chair. He started screaming as high and loud as his friend. I had to laugh. One minute they had been, by their own reckoning, big-time South London gangsters, ready to cut my throat on a Virgin flight to Florida, and the next they were a couple of screaming little babies looking for their mum.

The stewards hurried to the scene and combined forces to push me down the aisle. Impressive. They threatened to handcuff me with plastic ties and decided that the flight was going to be diverted to Canada, where I would be arrested for assault. 'You're in serious trouble here, mate. You'll be looking at jail time.'

I was still furious. 'Fine,' I said. 'Arrest me. I don't care. You're the ones with the problem here. You'll still be left with that pair of idiots, tormenting all the other passengers on this plane.'

But Ian kept his cool. 'This is an outrage!' he said to the cabin crew. 'This is disgusting. Your young crew allowed those idiots to get drunk, and they attacked us. You've obviously looked at your records, and seen that I'm a regular flyer. I understand you're training staff on this route, but they are inexperienced and are letting customers get drunk. We asked to be moved, and you didn't move us. And now you are blaming my friend for standing up for us.'

The families sitting in the area came on board too, telling the stewards that they had got the wrong guy, because the South London geezers had been the aggressors in the situation, not me. They all insisted that, if I was arrested, they would write to the airline and complain because, as they saw it, I had been standing up for the families with children who were being bullied by the two unruly idiots while the airline staff just kept fuelling their behaviour with more and more free booze.

'OK, fine,' the cabin crew eventually said. 'You can sit at the back of the plane and behave yourself.'

Ian tried to get us moved to the front, but that didn't work, so I did what I was told. The plane did not divert to Canada and we reached our destination more or less on schedule. At the back of the plane, away from the two morons I had taken out, I was able to relax a little and I started to calm down somewhat. From my vantage point, I could still see the pair of them. Having completely lost their drunken bravado, they were now crestfallen, staring at the floor while a doctor who happened to be on board sewed the first aggressor's ear back together. When we arrived in Florida, I was firmly instructed not to leave the plane until they had got off first.

Later, the two losers walked past us in the arrival lounge while we were speaking with the crew. They shuffled past me on their way out, reluctant even to make eye contact and clearly afraid that I was going to jump up and give them a second helping. The police were waiting just outside the airport and they were immediately arrested and deported back to Britain, because their plan was to drive away in their rental car, and they were clearly way too drunk to do anything of the sort.

Ian and I went on to have our holiday, and on the way home we were upgraded to Upper Class by Virgin Airlines, because the airline staff knew that they had screwed up. Flying Upper Class was fantastic, and I felt that it would be a nice thing to get used to.

'I should hit more people,' I commented to Ian cheerfully. 'Maybe I'll get a free car the next time. Or a free condo for a couple of weeks. It could turn into a nice little earner.' I laughed at my own joke.

'Don't you dare,' Ian replied. 'Don't even make jokes about it. It could easily have gone horribly wrong. You won't always be as lucky as this. Take my advice and keep your cool, because the next time you might really get into trouble and it could end up being a lot more difficult.'

'Go on, mate,' I said. 'I was just joking. There isn't going to be a next time.'

But Ian had no idea how prophetic his words would turn out to be.

10

GRIEVOUS
BODILY HARM

You can run away from your past, as I did the moment I left St Leonard's at the age of seventeen. But the past has a habit of jumping back out at you and tripping you up with memories when you least expect it, and when you are least able to deal with the consequences. Soon I was brought back to reality and to the memories that I had been trying so hard for so long to repress, with a resounding thud.

Not long after Ian and I returned from our holiday in Florida, I was briefly involved with a girl who turned out to be living in a fancy apartment in Hornchurch – in a complex that used to be St Leonard's, which had finally closed its doors as a children's home in 1985. The fashion was now for unwanted kids to be raised in much smaller living units, and places like St Leonard's were out of style.

When the children's home had finally ceased to function as such, the site had become an upmarket housing estate, and each of the cottages that had once housed up to thirty children at a time was subdivided into three luxury apartments. Because the home was set in attractive grounds and featured pretty Victorian architecture, it had become a rather desirable place to live and one of the more sought-after developments in the area. This woman brought me back to her place one night after we had been out on a date and, astonishingly, I found out that her bedroom was the exact same room that had once been my dormitory all those years before. Her bed was even in the precise spot where mine had once stood, although, of course, the room was completely unrecognisable as the rather grotty dormitory that I had known. From her living-room window, I could see over to the cottage where my best mate Liam had lived. I stood there for a moment and mimed a wave at the skinny child of my memories. I had not been in touch with Liam since I had left St Leonard's, but I thought about how he would have laughed at this scenario; me invited back to a girl's house only to find it was the home I had fled from all those years before.

The cottages were all snuggled into the same beautiful grounds that had witnessed so many miserable childhoods, and the avenues that wound around them bore names that recalled the former rulers of the fiefdom – 'Prescott Way', and so forth. I couldn't help but laugh. Imagine all these well-heeled residents living in an estate where a road might be named after a paedophile! If they only knew. What I did notice was that the cottage still felt just the same as it had when I was a kid, despite the expensive renovations. The old ghosts were still there.

It might sound as though destiny had meant for us to be together, but that wasn't the case, because this girl was a bit weird and I realised it almost as soon as I had met her. Perhaps the malevolent echoes of all those unhappy kids, all now long departed the home, with many having also departed this world, had gone to her head. She kept telling me that the fact that her apartment was the cottage where I had grown up showed we were meant to be united until death did us part. After just a few days, I realised that she was disturbed and that I would be much better off without her. When I tried to disentangle myself from what was promising to be a much less than satisfactory relationship, she took to parking her car outside my place and sitting there for hours in the dark, waiting and watching for me to come out. At one point, my mate Ian and I were hiding on the floor, running from one end of the house to the other to avoid her gaze as she looked from window to window. We were laughing, but it really wasn't funny any more and I just wanted it to end. When she eventually left, I found a large pile of presents on the doorstep. Our relationship, such as it was, had lasted for one week, and she stalked me for three more until I began to feel genuinely nervous. Whenever I was getting any grief from a man, I knew what to do. But I couldn't hit a girl, so I just didn't know what approach to take. Eventually, I had to threaten her, telling her that I would report her to the police and make sure she lost her job, so that she would back off.

Looking back, it seems almost as though this silly little episode was a reminder to me of where I had come from, lest I should grow too comfortable and confident with my newfound success and growing social confidence. Because, just around the corner, my past and the violent nature that had developed in me as a result of it were always waiting to trip me up and send me right back to where I had come from.

When I hit my early thirties, I came perilously close to losing everything I had worked so hard for, and to making an abrupt U-turn on the road I was travelling, heading all the way back to the wrong side of the tracks and the horrible destiny that Auntie Coral had so often predicted for me: 'You're rubbish. You'll never amount to anything. Look at you, you fucking retard. You Irish lowlife scum.

You're just a bloody Connolly, aren't you? Prison fodder from the day you were born, you little shit. Who ever loved you? Nobody, that's who... and nobody ever fucking will.'

My primary occupation at this time was working as a personal trainer. Although personal trainers are ten a penny nowadays, back in the late eighties/early nineties, they were a new phenomenon in the UK, and, as I said, I was, in fact, one of the first personal trainers in the UK. Although the media frenzy had died down somewhat and I was no longer appearing on television on a regular basis, things were continuing to go well for me professionally, and I was satisfied that my career was progressing quite nicely and that the service I offered was one that my clients both enjoyed and benefitted from. Also at the time, to make a little extra money, I was running the security for a little wine bar not very far from where I lived. The bar was very popular with a lot of serious people with equally serious commitments and responsibilities in a range of areas. In that closely knit community, everybody knew everybody, and security in the small two-storey wine bar was very tight, for obvious reasons. I only let in the customers who were the right people for that club and was strict in turning away anyone who was likely to cause trouble or attract the wrong sort of attention, or who didn't really know what sort of place they were trying to get into. Most of the time, people did as they were told and business was quite uneventful and a nice little earner to have on the side.

On this particular night, five friends of the doorman I was working with came up and tried to get in.

'Sorry, gentlemen,' I said, as nicely as I could. 'There's no room at the inn tonight. You'll just have to go somewhere else.'

'Come on,' they pleaded. 'Make an exception this once. We really want to go in. We won't cause any trouble, mate. Scout's honour.'

'No, guys, sorry,' I said. I could see that not only were they the wrong people for this particular club, but they were also well on their way to being outrageously drunk. Also, I had a sort of sixth sense that they were likely to cause trouble and that I would regret it if I gave in to their demands. You develop an instinct for that sort of thing after working on the doors for years.

'Come on,' my companion urged. 'They're my friends. Do me a favour and let them in. They are good guys. They won't cause any trouble. You can trust me, mate. I'll vouch for them.'

I looked at them. They looked back. It was against my better judgement, but I did not want to be on bad terms with my colleague. Life is too short to spend your evenings working the door with someone who is annoyed with you.

With more than a few misgivings, I stood aside

to let them in. 'All right, then. But, at the first sign of any trouble from you lot, you're out and you're not coming back. Got it?'

The five geezers barged past me like five chimpanzees on heat without so much as thanking me for my generosity. They were prize morons and the very first thing they did was to start causing trouble, as I had feared they would from the outset. They went straight up on the balcony, throwing lit fag butts from the balcony into girls' cleavages. The bar was equipped with a panic button that set off a flashing red light to alert doormen to any danger. I saw the light, went to investigate and found these five idiots tossing cigarettes over the balcony and laughing uproariously as they did so. They clearly had no idea of the trouble they could potentially find themselves in if they crossed the wrong people in a place like this.

'You're out,' I told them. 'You've got to go. I warned you when you asked to come in. Come on; fucking get outside now!'

'Oh yeah?' sneered one of the bozos. 'Like you are going to make us go? I don't think so, mate. There's five of us, pal, and last time I looked there was only one of you.'

I looked around for my companion, but he had disappeared, because he knew exactly what these geniuses were capable of. Somehow, despite being on my own, I managed to get them outside, but, as we walked through the door, one of them turned to me. 'I'll have it with you outside on the street.'

All I cared about at that moment was getting these five monkeys outside. The bar was packed, and I knew that if they exploded in there a lot of innocent people were going to get hurt. Glasses would be flying and people would be getting cut, and things would get very ugly very quickly.

I stood on the step and looked at them under the street lights. They were all drunk, belligerent and astonishingly stupid. They were a disaster waiting to happen. There were five of them and, with my colleague missing in action, only one of me. The queue of people waiting to get into the bar stood and gawked at the action, not realising that, with the situation as tense as it was, it was far from unlikely that they would get caught up in whatever was about to happen, and maybe even seriously hurt. I took one step forward, off the step, so that I could tell them to sober up and piss off home, because there was nothing for them here. I hoped that there was still a chance that they would go quietly.

Suddenly, one of the morons kicked my feet out from under me, and then all five were jumping on me and kicking me in the head as I lay on the pavement. I could hear their laughter and deep breathing as they gave it all they had.

As you can imagine, I had to make a snap

decision about what to do before I took some serious damage. There were five of these bastards, and I knew in a flash that, if I let them hurt me, if I let them keep the upper hand, I might be killed. Or worse – I could be left seriously disabled. That would mean I wouldn't be able to work. I wouldn't be able to do anything. Somehow, in the few seconds that passed between being knocked to the floor and the five monkeys trying to jump all over my head, I found time to think about Ronnie Redruff, an old doorman friend of mine whom I had known for years.

Ronnie Redruff was a former British heavy-weight champion and someone for whom I had always had a huge amount of respect. He was a rough guy, a real old-school doorman who had punched so much that his wrists were fucked, and been punched so much that his nose was permanently askew. Ronnie looked like the type of man you wouldn't want to mess with, and that's exactly what he was. But there was a lot more to Ronnie than just brawn. He was also a smart customer whose advice I tended to listen to, because he had been around the block more than a few times and knew a hell of a lot about human nature and how the world works. Some years before, Ronnie and I had worked on the door together at The Kings, which is one of the toughest pubs in Ilford. They had boxing on every night as well as strippers and blue comedians. It was a really rough house with tough customers who were liable to cause trouble and they needed a serious doorman to stop the whole thing from descending into bloody chaos. Ronnie worked with another big geezer called Lenny McLean who went by the nickname 'The Guv'nor'. As an aside, McLean went on to feature in *Lock, Stock and Two Smoking Barrels*; sadly he died of cancer aged just forty-nine. In his prime, he had been a monster of a man.

Anyway, as I lay there trying to deflect their blows and listening to their laughter and the horrified gasps of the customers queuing to get in, I remembered Ronnie's frequent advice: 'Paul, it's better to be tried by twelve than carried by six.'

What Ronnie meant was that, when the chips are down, you do what you have to do to survive and deal with the consequences afterwards because anything is better than being killed. It is never a good time to give up.

I knew that Ronnie was right and that I should take care of myself now and ask questions later. I've got to do something about this, I thought. I'm not going to be carried by six.

I was doing my best to parry the blows that seemed to be raining on me from all directions when, luckily, seemingly out of nowhere, one of the other doormen appeared on the scene and started dragging these idiots off me. I somehow managed to get to my feet and faced the bastards. They were all very drunk. That might help me. But there were still five of them, and only one of me.

'Think you're big men then, do you?' I said, wiping my own blood off my face with my sleeve. 'I'll have it with the fucking lot of you, you pricks.'

The mouthpiece of the little gang came at me, roaring and flailing his fists. I hit him with an upper cut as he tried to head-butt me. I took him sideways and he went up in the air. I took all his teeth out and left him on the floor, sprawling among the discarded ivories with his face pushed sideways against the cement. His friend came running at me and I put him through a glass door, leaving him in shreds and shrieking like a turkey the day before Christmas. I turned around to see where the others were, but all I could hear was the sound of their footsteps receding into the distance because they had seen what I had dished up to their friends, and they didn't want any of it for themselves. So they weren't a problem any more, or at least not for now. But I still had two men to deal with. They were wounded and they were also very angry and they were both getting back to their feet, planning to join forces so as to get their revenge on me.

The adrenaline rushed to my head, granting me strength and the will to take on two men at the same time, and I gave it to them both until they stopped punching back and fell to the ground. I will never know how one of them managed to get up again, because I was more determined than I had ever been before to stand up for myself and not to put myself in a vulnerable situation.

The other three ran away from the nightclub until they encountered some coppers. They told the police that their mates had just been beaten by a giant of a man, who was at least six foot four and heavily muscled with blond cropped hair. I am a lot shorter than that, and my hair is black, but the police didn't have any trouble identifying me, because my monkey suit was completely soaked in the blood of the two men I had taken out. When the police arrived, I didn't make any effort to conceal who I was or what I had done because I knew that I had just been doing my job and that, if I hadn't reacted as quickly, decisively and violently as I had, I would be seriously injured or even dead. I also knew that I had protected the people in the queue, any one of whom could have been caught up in the violence.

Unfortunately, the police did not see things the same way.

'You're in trouble now, mate,' I was told by a cheery-looking officer. 'You're coming with us.'

I was used to dealing with the Met in London and these were the suburban Essex coppers, who seemed to have a different rule book and not to understand the law of the street.

There and then, outside the nightclub with my hands slick with blood and my heart still beating fast from the exertion of defending myself, I was arrested and charged with Grievous Bodily Harm. Several of my attackers' teeth were still embedded in my knuckles and, while getting them there may have hurt them more than it hurt me, my hands were still smarting. My head was bleeding heavily, too, and I could already feel the swelling coming up. The police took a lot of photographs of my hands for their evidence. I could not fucking believe it. How had I let this happen? Things had been going so well for me. I had finally created a career that I could be justifiably proud of. I was building my own set of contacts. I had my own home in a pleasant part of Essex. I had a good network of friends and, increasingly, friends who had nothing to do with the dark world in which I had spent so much time living and working. I had begun, finally, to respect myself and my capabilities and, for the first time that I could remember, the voice of Auntie Coral, which had stayed with me every day, telling me how useless I was, had begun to recede.

Now I was up for a charge of GBH and GBH with Intent, and if I went down for either charge it meant a prison sentence and almost certainly the end of any respectable career. If I got done for GBH with Intent, it would mean a long sentence and a bad reputation that would follow me for the rest of my life. Either way, I would have a criminal record, which would mean that there would be no chance of working in any upmarket gym or health establishment and pretty much doom me to a life of not being qualified to do anything but work doors or in private security until I was too old and battered to do even that any more.

It would also mean that all the horrible things that Auntie Coral had said about me when I was a child were, in fact, true. That despite all my hard work; despite the fact that I had learned how to read and write and had become qualified in my field; despite my successes, my magazine articles and my experiences of working out the rich and famous; despite all that, I was a useless, stupid lump who had been inexorably bound for prison ever since the day that I was born. That there was something intrinsically wrong with me and that I had been doomed to this from the moment my mother had left me out with the rubbish because even then she had been able to see what sort of a misbegotten spawn I was.

The case took a year and a half to come to court; the worst eighteen months of my life and a time that I would do literally anything to avoid having to go through again. During that period, I had to appear at a magistrates' court on a regular basis and I couldn't leave the country without permission from the local police station. Because work was taking me overseas a lot at that time, I had to go to the police station often, which was both a pain in the arse and a constant reminder of the awful threat that was hanging over me. I couldn't do door work, because doormen have to be registered and cannot be in any trouble with the law. Security-wise I could run private security for dubious characters, but that was all.

The worst thing, however, was the waiting, the endless waiting. I would wake in the morning and think, Shit, I might be going down for GBH. I might be about to lose all that I have been working for all these years. This might be it. I tried to banish the thought as best I could by working so hard physically that I was exhausted in the evenings. Somehow, I would manage to avoid thinking about it and get to sleep. But it was still there, tormenting me, every time I woke in the morning, my very own sword of Damocles, taunting me with my past and with the prospect of a ruined future.

During this period, I took a trip to San Francisco to see Ian, who was living over there, ostensibly to help me to take my mind off things. As we enjoyed the good weather and the Californian food one beautiful afternoon, Ian suggested that we might do a tour of San Francisco Bay, including Alcatraz.

'You're having a laugh, aren't you?' I asked him. 'I could easily be seeing Alcatraz for real when I get home.'

'Oh, sorry, mate,' Ian said, immediately realising his gaffe.

But the day had been ruined for me; the thought of prison had been introduced, banishing everything else.

And then, all I could hear was Coral and Starling saying to me as they had said so many times, 'You are scum. You are a Connolly. You are in here because nobody wants you. You are abnormal. Why would you be in here otherwise? You would be at home with a normal family.'

Over the years, I had taken more beatings than I could remember. I had been stabbed and bitten, beaten and spat at. My body was covered in scars from all of these encounters, as it still is today. It was a roadmap that illustrated more than graphically how I had travelled from childhood to the present, from one violent encounter to another. I had often been asked by people gentler than me how it was that I seemed not to be traumatised by all the attacks and counterattacks I had suffered. The fact was that none of the beatings, stabbings or bites I ever took affected me in the slightest, compared to the mental torture I took from Auntie Coral for years. Over and over again, the woman who was supposed to be caring for me had eroded whatever confidence and self-respect I might otherwise have had. The worst thing is that mental torture is the hardest to prove, and the easiest to get away with. The beatings, bites and stabbings? They had never really bothered me much at all. In fact, in a strange way, I had almost enjoyed them, because surviving and becoming stronger despite being hurt was testimony to my ability to survive almost anything and made me feel that, just perhaps, I would come out on top in the end.

But now the thought that maybe Auntie Coral had been right about me all along stayed with me all day long and accompanied me to bed at night. There were few people to whom I could talk about it, but my mate Ian came through for me. Ian, who worked in the area of Information Technology, was not even remotely involved in my world, so I could tell him things that couldn't be voiced elsewhere. Ian is a classy, university-educated guy from a good family. To say that he has a different perspective from me on things is putting it mildly. He was unlike most of my friends, who were tough guys like me. It was good to have someone who could give me a fresh way of looking at things.

Ian kept telling me that Auntie Coral had been wrong about me and trying to assure me that things would work out all right in the end because he knew and I knew that I hadn't done anything inappropriate in a situation in which my own life was very much on the line. I appreciated his efforts to provide solace. But it was very difficult for me to have faith in his words as I waited for my trial date to be announced.

When my case finally came up in Crown Court, it took a week to be heard. One long, stressful, awful week that I never want to have to go through again. The only good thing about the start of that week was that it meant that the waiting was finally over. Whatever was about to happen, at least I would know my fate.

When you are in trouble, you learn who your real friends are. I had a pal called Ray Tame who ran the door at a nightclub called Palms. Ray was getting on a bit in years by then, but even then I still wouldn't have wanted to fight him – and I was prepared to take on almost anybody. He is a big, tough guy who does not ask questions or take any prisoners. Ray came to court for me every day and gave evidence in my defence.

'I've worked with Paul on many occasions,' Ray said. 'I've seen him being spat at and provoked and he's never reacted with anything but professionalism. Paul is not a violent character. Paul wouldn't have taken them out if he didn't have to. It was a question of defending himself from attack.'

But the prosecuting barrister kept harping on about how I should have walked away: 'Why didn't you just go? Why didn't you just put the aggressors outside and leave them there? You didn't have to fight them. You didn't have to get involved. You could have been the bigger man, and just left them there...'

Ray, who had run security courses for the government and was a court bailiff, explained on my behalf, 'There was a queue of customers outside the door. Anybody who knows anything about security work realises that Mr Connolly had a primary responsibility to the people in the queue at the front of the premises. He couldn't walk back in; he had to stay outside to protect the people in the queue, because, in a situation like that, any one of them could have been hurt. And that would have meant that Mr Connolly had failed to do his job properly.'

As Ray spoke, I could see the jury nodding and an understanding beginning to dawn on their faces, and I began to have some hope that maybe, just maybe, things would go my way. I did feel confident that I had not done the wrong thing. It was true that I had hurt two men very badly. It was also true that the encounter had started with them and their three friends jumping on my head.

Ray didn't just know about security work; he was also very knowledgeable about the law, thanks to his work as a court bailiff. He was able to use all this information; he was able to make the jury see the situation from the viewpoint of a doorman. He was able to make them understand that the people who had attacked me were bullies who could have lashed out at anyone and that, if I had not defended myself, I might very well have been killed by them, while any of the customers waiting in the queue outside the club could have been badly hurt. While my actions might not have been nice and while they might not have been gentle, they were very necessary.

Further support came from strange places. I have already mentioned the various policewomen I had been involved with over the years. Anthea, the woman I had been going out with at the time of the assault, came to give evidence at the court case. Anthea and I had since split up, but she was a good friend for me during the trial, and she wasn't afraid to put herself on the line on my behalf. Speaking as a police officer, Anthea gave a long statement saying that, in her view, I had not been dealt with in the correct way by her colleagues in uniform. I had been straight with the police about what had happened and what my role in it had been.

I owe Anthea a lot for turning up on my behalf and telling the truth to the jury and the rest of the court, not least because our relationship had ended some time before, and I was already seeing someone else. I will always be grateful to Anthea for coming through for me.

Because of the type of people I had come to know, I was able to call on friends who worked in blue-chip organisations who were able to come and give character references for me. As well as Anthea, several friends with upstanding reputations and sterling CVs came and testified that I was a good bloke, and I think that the judge was surprised by the calibre of my friends.

As the trial drew near to an end, I was taken out from the cells and placed in front of the court and jury to hear my fate. I had been dreaming – mostly nightmares, of course – about this moment for the last eighteen months. Now that it was actually happening, it didn't quite seem real. I thought that I had reason to hope a little bit, but how much? It was very hard for me to tell how things would go. I didn't want to give in to hope, only for hope to be dashed to the ground when I was sent away.

Every time defendants come into the court, they are frisked to make sure that they are not carrying anything that could serve as a missile to throw at the judge. On this particular day, they forgot to search me and, as I stood there while the judge was deliberating, just before summing up the case and making his final statement, my phone went off in my pocket: 'Pump up the volume, pump up the volume.'

As I fumbled to turn it off, the jury started to laugh. My hands were trembling too much to turn it off and it kept on ringing. It seemed to get louder and louder.

'Pump up the volume, pump up the volume.'

'Why has that man got a phone on him?' the judge asked severely. 'He could have thrown it at me. There are rules against such things for a reason, you know.'

'Pump up the volume, pump up the volume.'

The police took the phone from me as quickly as they could reach me, but they couldn't figure out how to turn it off, so they brought it into a nearby cell and left it there. The ringtone echoed inside, magnifying it until the sound completely dominated the courtroom.

'Pump up the volume, pump up the volume.'

Still the police couldn't turn it off and by now the jury and even the lawyers were almost in hysterics.

Shit, I thought, this isn't helping my case at all. The judge was looking thunderous.

Eventually, the phone got turned off and the judge continued, but he did not look happy. He summed up efficiently and sent the jury out to do their deliberations.

The case had lasted from Monday to Friday, and the jury went out at lunchtime on Friday to discuss my case and decide my fate. Earlier, my barrister had been giving me some plain talking. It seemed that he was less impressed with the hope that Ray had injected into the proceedings than I had been.

He went on to advise me of alternative strategies in the light of the proceedings. He explained that if I admitted to Section 20 – Grievous Bodily Harm – I would receive a lesser prison sentence. If I accepted this charge, I could avoid a Section 18 – GBH with Intent, a much more serious crime. I was stubborn, though; I had done nothing wrong and didn't see why I should admit to something of which I was not guilty.

'No fucking way,' I said. 'I didn't do anything wrong and I'm not going to stand here and say that I did.'

I looked down at my hands, which held tightly on to the edge of the desk. My knuckles were white with tension. I could see that my hands were trembling, but I could do nothing to control them. Still, there was no way on earth I was going to plead guilty. I had spent my whole life trying to stand up for myself whenever I found myself facing a bully, and I was not about to stop doing that now that I was facing this new challenge and the devastating prospect of several years behind bars and the loss of all the things I had worked so hard to achieve.

The jury stayed out for an hour, which is a very short period for deliberation. It didn't feel short to me, though; that was the longest hour of my life. But, when they filed back in, they were all smiling and looking quite relaxed. I remembered that I had been told that a smiling jury never convicts. I felt another glimmer of hope.

We all rose to listen to the verdict. The foreman of the jury stood.

'Have you reached a unanimous verdict on both charges?'

'Yes, your honour, we have.'

By now I was cacking myself big time.

'In the case of the charge of Mr Connolly, Section 20, Grievous Bodily Harm, how do you find?'

'Not guilty.'

You could have heard a pin drop in the court. I had been found not guilty for GBH, but that made it more likely that I would be found guilty of the more serious charge, which would mean a minimum of five years in prison.

'In the case of the charge of Mr Connolly, Section 18, Grievous Bodily Harm with Intent to commit Grievous Bodily Harm, how do you find?'

'Not guilty.'

Not guilty!

I had been so convinced that I was going to be found guilty and sent away to serve the prison sentence that Auntie Coral had convinced me was hanging over my head, I didn't hear the word 'not' and for an awful moment my heart sank and I began to look around for the coppers who were going to take me away.

But then a great cheer broke out in the gallery as my friends and supporters rose to their feet, clapping and cheering.

Well, they can't be cheering if I am going to prison, I thought. Perhaps everything is OK after all …

The judge said, 'You are free to go, Mr Connolly,' and added, 'This case has been a waste of taxpayers' money. If you had been walking in the street rather than working on the door when five men attacked you, it would never have come to trial at all.'

I was so relieved that it didn't occur to me to thank the jury or the judge for the outcome of my trial. I ran out of the courtroom as quickly as possible. The men I had beaten up outside the club had not been able to take me out, but the waves of emotion that crashed over me now certainly did. Suddenly unable to bear my own weight, I collapsed on to the floor in the corridor outside, and one of my friends had to pick me up off the floor and help me to stand straight as I gathered my emotions. The sudden relief of the stress that had been weighing me down for a full year and a half was almost more than I could bear, and I felt overcome with exhaustion of a sort that I had never experienced before.

The jury had found that when I beat those men I had been acting in self-defence, and I used reasonable force. In the circumstances, my violence had to exceed theirs because, if it hadn't, there would have been a real, serious risk that I could have been killed. I should never have been arrested in the first place and fifty thousand pounds of taxpayers' money had gone down the drain.

Being found not guilty of committing Grievous Bodily Harm and Grievous Bodily Harm with Intent was a real turning point in my life because not only had I come up against the genuine risk of spending an extended period in prison with all the associated losses and damages to my career, but I had had to confront my deepest fear – that everything Auntie Coral and Starling had said about me during the course of all those years was actually true.

I told myself that I would no longer put myself in the sort of situations in which such things were likely to happen. I resolved that, from then on, I would be the sort of person of whom I could be proud.

After that, I stopped doing door work, concentrated wholly on my career as a personal trainer and I turned my back on anything that was seedy and underhand, or flirted with illegality or with violence. I promised myself that things would be different from now on and that I would keep my temper in check.

Perhaps it was because of the turning over of a new leaf and my decision to stay away from sticky situations, but, shortly after the trial, I got back in contact with Mary for the first time in almost twenty years. I think that I wanted to show her that I had turned out all right, despite everything. I had often thought about Mary in the intervening years, but I had never contacted her because I had a feeling that she would not have been particularly proud of the sort of person I had become since she had last seen me at the age of twelve or thirteen. I also suspected that she would not have approved of the type of people with whom I had mixed. Once I had decided to definitively draw a line under that way of life, I started to wonder how Mary was and to remember how she had been a beacon of hope for me in an otherwise desolate childhood. I wrote a letter to an address that I found on a letter I had received from her many years earlier. Mary had moved to another house in the meantime, but the letter was duly forwarded and contact was renewed.

I learned that Mary had been through some tough times of her own. She had broken her back in a car accident, and wasn't able to ride her horses any more. But she was making the best of things and getting on with life.

'So what are you doing, Paul?' Mary asked.

'I'm the head personal trainer for the David Lloyd clubs in Essex and the South East.'

Mary was silent.

'Is something wrong?'

'No,' she said. 'It's just that Spencer's a personal trainer too and he's the head personal trainer for the David Lloyd clubs on the south coast.'

Perhaps all those games of tennis I had played with Mary as a child had more of an influence on the choices I made than I thought.

Mary and I talked for a long time, and I was very happy to realise that our old bond had not been broken. After all, she had been the closest thing to a real mother figure that I had ever had, and that sort of affection runs deep. I told Mary about my successes in boxing, and the accident that had cut my boxing career short. Spencer had a boxing background too. The parallels between our lives were almost eerie. I had often wondered how my life would have turned out if I had really become Mary's adopted son. If Spencer is anything to go by, some parts of mine are likely to have been very similar, although, of course, Spencer had never done some of the nastier things that I did, or worked in the shadows as I had done for so many years.

It was wonderful to know that I had escaped the prison sentence that seemed to have been hanging over me not just since the incident at the nightclub, but since birth. It was wonderful to have renewed contact with the one woman who had shown me throughout my childhood that women could be kind and nurturing, generous and gracious. Finally,

I could sense a sort of calming of the disturbed waters of my soul. Now in my mid-thirties, it seemed that I was entering a new, happier period of my life and that I might be able to continue moving onwards and upwards.

But I didn't realise that another and very significant turning point lay just ahead.

11

THE MAPPERTON CASE

I had not answered the door when the cops came around first because, two weeks earlier, I had been involved in a road-rage incident and had knocked out an off-duty copper. My old anger still simmered beneath the surface, and my resolve to avoid situations that might conceivably lead to violence didn't have a clause to deal with the rude, aggressive drivers I seemed to come up against on a regular basis. This man had deserved the dig he took, but, as cops always stand up for each other, I had been concerned that there might be repercussions and afraid that the two women officers on my doorstep meant that there could be a spot of trouble ahead. Having just been found innocent of a charge of GBH, getting into legal difficulties again was the last thing I wanted.

What had happened was this: a driver behind me in a fast car with a girl he was trying to impress had been driving right up behind me on an Essex road flashing his lights and generally being annoying. Remembering my promise to myself to avoid getting into the sort of situations that could become difficult, I pulled over into the slow lane to let him past, but the idiot wouldn't go; he just kept driving right behind me, flashing the headlights and making gestures that I couldn't quite make out but that I suspected were obscene.

I stopped at the traffic lights, and so did he. He jumped out of his car and started to approach me with a swagger. That was enough. I had been as patient as possible for a man with a short fuse. I got out of my car, closed the door and faced him. I could see that he had something in his hand, and I certainly did not want to be the first to get hit, so I punched him hard and he fell heavily on to the ground while his girlfriend looked on, shrieking and wobbling on her high heels.

Then I saw that the thing in his hand was a luminous police jacket.

Fuck, I thought. Great fucking timing. This was the last thing I needed at this particular point in my life.

The policeman came around and staggered to his feet. 'You're in trouble, mate,' he said. 'I'm going to read you your rights.' He got me into a bear hug.

'Mate, I'm leaving,' I said. 'You provoked me

and I'm pretty sure I haven't done anything much wrong here. Let go of me.'

He wouldn't let go so I head-butted him, left him groaning on the floor and drove off.

When I left to get petrol the next morning, about twenty police officers surrounded me and nicked me for assaulting a police officer. They took me down to Romford Police Station where I was greeted with outright hilarity, because the man I had hit had been an Essex copper, and the Romford boys are not fond of the Essex police.

'Look,' I was told, 'this guy was an idiot. He's a young copper and he was trying to show off in front of this girl and, when he saw you speeding or whatever it was, he wasn't even on duty and had no right to do anything. This isn't going to go any further. Trust me. This will be dealt with. He's in serious shit because he was overstepping his remit.'

In fact, I even got an apology from the coppers and a letter saying that there wouldn't be any more action.

But then these two women police officers came and would not go away. They just kept coming and knocking on my door and trying to peer in through the front window. They would leave, and then come back. They would stand and wait, talking quietly among themselves. This happened many times, and, as I assumed that they had come because of the incident with the copper, I didn't answer the door because I just didn't want to know about it. But then I realised that they must have been there for some other reason, although I had no idea what it might be.

Eventually, as you know, I let them in.

When they told me that a big investigation was ongoing into the abuses at St Leonard's, I was deeply shocked, because it had never occurred to me that anyone would ever be punished for what they had done or that I would ever find myself in an encounter with the coppers in which they were doing their best to be kind and to make me feel at ease.

While, of course, I was pleased that perhaps the men and women who had done so much damage to so many children would finally get in trouble for their crimes, I also learned that most of the kids I had grown up with were dead, many years before their time, and that, awful as my childhood had been, many of the others – including my best mate Liam – had it a lot worse than me. I learned that I had not even realised quite how bad things had been at St Leonard's. I had thought that I had been living through hell, but I hadn't even known the half of it. All of us kids had known about the sexual contact between the adolescent children and the caregivers, and obviously we had known about the violence and abuse, because we had all suffered it to varying degrees. But now I learned that the abuse had been more widespread, more organised and more sinister than I had ever realised. So much so that many of the kids who had grown up in the home had found life too intolerable to continue with and had decided to end it, in one way or another.

Apparently, the first formal complaints against the abusers had been made in the mid-1990s by someone who had been there at the same time as me, but it had taken some time for the investigators to uncover enough evidence to bring the case to trial. It would take a couple of years for the case to come to court. Meanwhile, anyone who had survived their experiences of St Leonard's and now learned that many of their childhood friends had not would just have to learn how to cope with a massive dose of survivor's guilt.

They hit me with everything: 'Were you in St Leonard's children's home? Are you Paul Connolly? We've got some bad news for you, I'm afraid. All the children you grew up with are dead, except for one, and he's in prison.' Despite the fact that several of my girlfriends had been police officers, I had always tended to see the coppers as enemies who couldn't be trusted and who should generally be avoided as much as possible. Now I realised that they could be human too.

Everything slowed down and I felt as though I was leaving my body. With a couple of sentences, the women police officers had taken me back twenty years. Almost all the people I had thought were living their lives somewhere, and possibly doing better than me, were dead.

Dead!

For years, I had deliberately pushed any thought of the children I had grown up with to the back of my mind. I had chosen to assume that things were OK for them, that somewhere out there Liam and the rest of them had jobs and houses, and wives and kids and dogs they took for walks – normal, pleasant, unremarkable lives. I had hoped, vaguely, that they were living better lives than mine. Now I had to confront the reality, which was that, as grim and gritty and difficult as my life had often been over the years, I was one of the lucky ones. I was one of the survivors.

The case against the former care workers of St Leonard's would take place in two parts. First there was a criminal prosecution taken by the state. Only later could a civil action on the part of the victims occur. The criminal prosecution was supposed to establish the guilt or innocence of the various people who had been accused, and lay the ground for any compensation cases that would be taken against the London Borough of Tower Hamlets Council.

Sadly, the criminal prosecution was a bit of a fiasco, despite the fact that many of the former residents of the homes gave statements, some in court. The witnesses were brave. Some of the people who had suffered the most as children now had to face their demons and lay their secrets bare in front of the jury at the Old Bailey in London. It must have been painfully difficult. On 23 January 2001, one of the local newspapers, the *Braintree and Witham Times*, published the following about the harrowing ordeal of one of the former victims of Uncle Bill:

A woman sobbed at the Old Bailey as she told how she was raped by William Starling while resident in an Essex children's home.

Weeping uncontrollably, the alleged victim, now 38, said she didn't reveal her terrible ordeal at the time because she thought no one would believe her and she would be 'locked away'.

She said the attack happened when she was ten or 11 years old. She left the home shortly afterwards but the abuse continued, she claimed.

The slim blonde revealed how Starling, now aged 74, of Rantree Fold, Basildon, would visit her at her parents' address and indecently assault her.

He is also alleged to have attacked her siblings as well as eight other children.

'Bill would give my mum some money to go shopping down the market and give my dad some money to go and have a drink at the pub,' she continued.

Once alone with her she said Starling would indecently assault her.

Afterwards she claimed he would sneer at her: 'No one will believe you, you are just a disturbed kid.'

She said that the rape happened in a shed in the back garden of the children's home.

Starling, the retired children's home worker, is said to have sexually abused 12 'vulnerable' children over a 20-year period. Miss Sally Howes, prosecuting, told the jury he carried out a 'cynical and calculated catalogue of abuse' while employed by the London Borough of Tower Hamlets.

Starling has pleaded not guilty to 25 sexual assaults, including three rapes, four counts of other serious sexual assaults, and 17 of indecent assault and indecency with a child.

After a long trial and the courageous disclosures of other victims of Bill Starling, Alan Prescott and some of their colleagues, the case finally ended. The outcome of it was reported as follows in the *Recorder* newspaper on 12 October 2001:

Two former workers at St Leonard's care home in Hornchurch have been jailed for sexually assaulting youngsters in two separate hearings at The Old Bailey.

Former magistrate Alan Prescott, 62, who was in charge of St Leonard's care home for 15 years, was jailed for two years on Friday for abusing boys.

Prescott's sentence was dreadfully brief, in light of all the damage he had caused to so many young lives. One cannot help but wonder if his position as a local magistrate helped him out. Bill Starling, however, received a longer sentence:

Prescott's jailing follows that of William Starling, 74, who was sentenced to 14 years jail at the Old Bailey last April. Court restrictions however have prevented the Recorder *from printing the details until Prescott was sentenced.*

Prescott had admitted to a number of cases of assault, but, when I was in the home, we were all confident that his inappropriate relationships with young boys were much more numerous than the four that he admitted to:

Last Friday, Prescott, who lives in Stepney, East London, admitted that he too had been abusing boys in his care, pleading guilty to sexually assaulting four victims between 1970 and 1980.

Almost hilariously, Prescott's dominant position in

his local community seems to have been cited by his legal counsel as a point in his favour, as if the abuse of trust of his position did not make what he had done even worse than it already was:

> He was described by his solicitor as a 'pillar of the community' and commanded great respectability.
>
> The social worker was a Havering magistrate for 24 years, a Labour councillor in Harold Hill and chief executive of an East London charity.
>
> He joined St Leonard's in 1968 and became superintendent in 1976, remaining in charge until it closed almost nine years later. But by the time he was in charge, he had already started abusing his position.
>
> The pervert plied one victim with drink before abusing him and even offered to help another with a court case in return for sex.
>
> Prosecutor Sally Howes told the court how Prescott first struck in 1970, sneaking into a 15 year old's dormitory before performing a sex act on him.
>
> He was finally arrested when police investigated allegations of a spate of abuse at St Leonard's.

Several of the charges against Prescott were never heard by the court, presumably because of a lack of evidence after the passage of so many years or, perhaps, because the boys he had taken advantage of had grown into the men who were so wounded and distressed that they had ended up taking their own lives and were no longer available to give evidence about what had happened to them as children. This meant that Prescott never faced trial for some of the crimes he had been accused of:

He pleaded guilty to four counts of indecent assault, but additional charges of six indecent assaults and one of buggery were ordered to lie on file.

Sentencing Prescott, Judge Jeremy Roberts told him: 'These offences are aggravated by the fact that you were in a position of power, authority and trust over your victims.'

'You were a figure of authority in the community and it's most unfortunate that behind the outward appearance of respectability, you were behaving in this kind of way towards the people in your charge.'

Particularly galling to learn was the fact that Prescott served very little time for the serious crimes that he had committed while the children he had abused would have to live with their memories forever:

Prescott has already spent 14 months on

remand so he will be released from prison shortly. He will be forced to sign on the sex offenders' registry for 10 years.

I was upset to learn that Prescott had received what was effectively a slap on the wrist for what had been very serious crimes.

While Alan Prescott's main interest in life had been adolescent boys, Bill Starling found himself in more serious trouble, largely because of the lower age profile of his victims and, perhaps, because most of them had been girls:

In the other court case Starling, known as 'Uncle Bill', subjected 11 children as young as five to a 'cynical and calculated catalogue of abuse' spanning two decades.

The court heard how 74-year-old Starling, from Basildon, targeted problem kids at the Tower Hamlets run home...

His horrific spree of abuse ran from the mid-1960s to the 1980s, and his victims included three members of the same family.

He moved from child to child when the elder victims became too old for his perverted tastes, abusing two sisters and a brother...

...He bribed a number of victims with 'money and cigarettes' to make them comply with his twisted demands, and he raped an 11-

year-old girl in a garden shed as she returned from a swimming session in the home.

Prosecutor Sally Howes told the court: 'There is a noticeable similarity of background to all these complainants at their time of residence at either St Leonard's or in Basildon.'

'They all had difficulties of one sort or another. Some had already been the victims of sexual abuse, others were emotionally damaged by either cruel, uncaring parents or parents who, due to inadequacies of their own, were simply unable to cope with the responsibility of bringing up their children.'

Starling was convicted of 19 sexual offences relating to eleven victims – nine girls and two boys. There was one offence of buggery, two rapes, one indecency with a child and 15 indecent assaults.

He was acquitted of one count of buggery and two indecent assaults, with a further count of buggery ordered to lie on file.

Judge Jeremy Roberts sentenced Starling to 10 years for each rape and the buggery, to run concurrently. He received two years for the first seven counts of indecent assault, concurrent to each other but consecutive to the 10 years.

For the remaining eight indecent assaults and the indecency with a child, he was sentenced to two years, concurrent with each

*other, but consecutive to the other sentences –
totalling 14 years.*

*The Judge told him: 'It's obvious from the
jury's verdict there came a stage when you fell
prey to the temptation to behave in an
inappropriate way towards these children.'*

*'When you found you got away with it, one
thing led to another, and you ended up
committing this catalogue of offences.'*

The newspaper also reported that the investigation
was still ongoing:

*The St Leonard sex abusers were finally brought
to justice thanks to the courage and persistence
of the Met Police's Operation Mapperton and
investigations are still going on.*

*The offences first came to light in 1995/6
when a complaint was made by one individual
who said that he had been abused at the
Hornchurch home.*

*Police set up an inquiry team called Operation
Harmon and their evidence was sent to the
Crown Prosecution Service, but it was decided
that there wasn't enough evidence to prosecute.*

*The same individual who had made the
original complaint continued to pester the police,
however, and in 1998 Operation Mapperton was
set up.*

A huge debt of gratitude is owed to the first person to speak out and complain about his experiences at St Leonard's because, without this initial complaint, it is very unlikely that anything would ever have been done to bring the aggressors to justice. Following his initial accusations, once the wheels started to turn, more and more former residents of the homes were interviewed, including me, and the truth had begun to emerge despite the fact that the authorities had apparently never kept proper records:

The lack of records by Tower Hamlets' social services department caused police problems, but talking to each former child at the home quickly opened many more doors.

From speaking to the former children, now adults, and many with their own families, it quickly became clear that Starling was a major suspect.

The team worked tirelessly, taking 360 statements and travelling across the country to interview victims. In October 1999 Starling was arrested and questioned, but from day one until the present day he has denied any wrongdoing.

It became clear from the statements that Starling wasn't the only one involved and soon Alan Prescott was questioned and arrested. There was a pattern to their victims; Starling's being of both sexes and aged five to 14, and Prescott's adolescent boys.

Det Con Ken Roast, part of the Operation Mapperton team, said: 'It was quite easy for them in their positions of authority, and they were helped by the fact that they were 15 miles down the road from their controlling authority Tower Hamlets.

'They wanted to be treated as their own little independent self-sufficient unit, and they knew that no one would believe the children if they told the truth.'

He said that the calibre of the evidence by the victims in court had been first class. He said the prosecution had expected some to crumble but they stood up admirably.

Apparently, quite a few of the children who had grown up in St Leonard's went to court to watch their former abusers receive their sentences:

Many were in court for the sentencing, and welcomed Starling's 14-year sentence, but were disappointed with the two years handed to Prescott, although apparently this was in line with sentences given in the 1970s, which judges have to take into account.

The article also stated that:

Det Con Roast doesn't believe Tower Hamlets are to blame for the scandal, pointing the finger at the individuals responsible for employing the sex beasts in the first place. He said that another worker had been sentenced to 18 months for buggery in 1981, and yet there was no internal investigation. The person also continued to work for Tower Hamlets.

In the same edition of the local paper, a detailed report of the assault of one of the formers residents was described in the context of that individual's struggle to have the names changed on the streets that now honoured the former abusers:

A victim of abuse at St Leonard's is leading a campaign to have Prescott Close, which was named after convicted former home boss Alan Prescott, renamed.

The victim, who cannot be named, was abused by Starling. He went to the home when he was just five and was one of the last people to leave when it closed, aged 18.

Starling would threaten to send the youngster 'to the funny farm' unless he succumbed to his sickening advances, and told him no one would believe him if he tried to tell the truth.

He gave evidence against Starling at the Old

Bailey, which he said had lifted a massive weight from his shoulders, and he is now trying to have the name of the road in which the home formerly stood changed...

The victim said that Starling was a very cunning man who would play on what the children feared the most in order to get his way.

He said that one minute he would be nice, saying he wanted to keep him at the home, and the next minute he would be acting like 'an animal', threatening to get rid of him.

People made statements about Starling, he said, but no one believed them. Once they did complain to social services, but when they came to question Starling he already knew of the youngsters' allegations and had come up with an excuse.

It was only when police approached him in the late 90s and told him that they believed him, that the victim was able to open his heart to the catalogue of abuse.

He said: 'I used to suffer from paranoia and thought people were talking about me behind my back. People wouldn't believe us back in those days, so why should they believe us now? We were brought up to think we were liars and no one cared, then all of a sudden the police came along and said they did believe us. It was amazing.'

The Mapperton case had involved testimony from hundreds of the former residents of St Leonard's. For the first time, someone had been willing to listen to us. It turned out that some of the cottages in the home had been worse than others, and that Bill Starling had been pretty much the leader of a paedophile ring that had been operating with impunity for years, wreaking havoc on the bodies and psyches of the children in question. Bill was the only aggressor who got anything like a substantial prison sentence, although fourteen years isn't a lot for what he did. The police had cocked up some of the investigation and they admitted as much, but there wasn't that much that could be done about it at this late stage in the day. The women police officers who had called around to my house had more or less admitted that there had been problems with the investigation from the outset and that the police had lost important evidence that could no longer be found. Prescott had already been in prison on remand and had served most of his sentence, so now he was due to get out.

After the case was heard, it got some coverage in the national press, perhaps most notably in an article in the *Guardian*, originally published on 24 October 2001, that I still find painfully difficult to read, because it describes in plain and horrifying language what had happened in the cottage opposite mine and describes the truth behind the suicide of the man whom I had once loved as a brother and from whose life I had departed all those years ago, when I left the children's home for the last time:

Nestling in the Essex countryside, the St Leonard's children's home should by rights have been a mini Utopia for the 300-odd youngsters in its care. With its 13 'cottages', each housing up to 30 children, its own hospital, church, school, swimming pool and gymnasium, and generous avenues set amid 86 acres, the late Victorian 'village' appeared a world away from the squalid council blocks where many of its residents had previously lived in the east London borough of Tower Hamlets.

'It was potentially idyllic,' says Seamus Carroll, who lived there with his brothers from the age of four, in the mid-1960s, until age 17. 'We always said, when we were growing up, it would be a wonderful place to be – if it were not for the staff, that is.'

For St Leonard's, which saw 3,000 children pass through its doors between 1965 and its closure in 1984, was a haven not for children, but for paedophiles who meted out abuse while purportedly providing the children's care... the lifting of reporting restrictions at the Old Bailey meant the full scale of the abuse could be, if not exposed, then at least hinted at. In a revelation largely banished from the news by the start of the bombing of Afghanistan, it emerged that one former house parent, Bill Starling, had indecently assaulted, raped or buggered 11 victims – aged from just five to 14 – over a 20-year period. Another defendant, the home's superintendent, Alan Prescott, a former JP, Labour councillor, Assistant Director of Social Services in Tower Hamlets and, later, chief executive of East End charity Toynbee Hall, had indecently assaulted four teenage boys at various points throughout the 1970s...

...Police believe that figures for the numbers of victims – 12 on the original indictment for Starling and seven for Prescott – may not be the full extent of the abuse, however. Daniel O'Malley, the detective inspector heading the continuing investigation, suggests there may have been as many as 70 victims – with 30 abused by Starling alone.

Nor do the figures adequately convey the legacy of the abuse, nor the culture of despair and secrecy that enabled the supposed carers to perpetuate the abuse with impunity.

'There was a complete conspiracy of silence,' says Carroll, now 40, the man who prompted the police investigation when he finally made a complaint to Tower Hamlets about the abuse he says he suffered from four to 15. 'As kids, we

never spoke about it to one another because of the sense of shame, the guilt, and the feeling of helplessness, and the staff who weren't involved turned a blind eye and pretended not to notice. The few children who tried to challenge them were threatened with Borstal, and when I did finally tell someone, he did nothing about it, because he was involved with teenage girls at the home himself.'

One of the original charges against Prescott – again dropped because of the loss of video evidence – also alleged that he indecently assaulted a boy who went to him for help against another abuser.

It wasn't until I read this article that I found out that Auntie Coral and that friend of hers had not been the only female abusers at St Leonard's, but that the situation had been awful in Myrtle Cottage, just opposite my cottage, too. That meant that my mate Liam, and many of the other kids in Myrtle Cottage, had been suffering untold horrors all the time I was at St Leonard's:

At first, the abuse came from a perhaps unexpected quarter – his house mother, who died before police began investigating in 1995 and so evaded prosecution. 'It was almost instantaneous,' says Carroll. 'It started with her

fondling us, and she was very persistent –
waking us in the night and touching our genitals
under the ruse of putting us on the potty.

'*She would do it to the girls as well as the*
boys, and she picked on the most vulnerable. We
were so young that any affection seemed better
than no affection. There was a sense that it was
better to be touched than not touched at all.'

The article goes on to describe the dreadful abuses
that Seamus suffered, and the absolute failure of
the authorities to do anything whatsoever to help
him. It also describes some of the dreadful things
that happened in Wallis Cottage, where I lived:

And, all the time, the abuse was being secretly
meted out elsewhere – at Wallis Cottage,
opposite Myrtle, where Starling would bribe his
female victims with money and cigarettes for
sex and brutally rape the boys while telling
them no one would believe the tales of such
'*problem children*'. *Prescott, as head of St*
Leonard's, had the power to root out the abuse
but instead did nothing.

Seamus also described the absolute power that the
house parents all had over the cottages in which they
worked, and the extremely unhealthy atmosphere
that reigned:

Carroll says: 'We were all suffering, but suffering alone because each house was a world unto itself. We lived in an atmosphere in which we were just like meat. When I searched for my files, I kept seeing notes like 'he's a pretty child' or 'he's an ugly child'.

Worst of all, the article revealed exactly what had happened to Seamus's younger brother, Liam, and to the rest of his family when they grew up and left home:

Carroll says that the legacy of such an upbringing has 'devastated' his family. One brother [Liam] flung himself in front of a high-speed train two years ago after being haunted for five years by rape flashbacks.

After the court case, my brother Declan and I got in touch to talk things over. He had been contacted as well and had also been asked to give a statement. We agreed to meet up and go and read our files together, a decision that had also been taken by many of the other former residents of St Leonard's. The files of all the kids who had grown up in St Leonard's had been made available at a special centre in East London, in a large room with social workers and counsellors standing by, in case anyone got upset or out of hand.

Whatever reaction they were expecting, I doubt the social workers anticipated the gales of laughter that came from Declan and myself. My file was enormous, because I had been in care from the age of two weeks right up to early adulthood. Declan's wasn't quite as big as mine, but it was still fairly substantial.

I laughed so hard reading my file that I had to sit down. By now, I knew that Bill Starling was serving time for what he had done and Alan Prescott had also served a little time. Knowing that the reports had been written by convicted paedophiles gave them a sort of black humour that just reduced me to tears of laughter.

'Paul is a very small child,' my file read. 'He has a bad temper and has trouble controlling himself. He is a violent boy who is expected to continue to have problems as he grows up.'

It was hilarious! I was very small, and the reason why was that I was malnourished. We all were, because the money for our food was routinely stolen.

Funniest of all was a note in Coral's hand: 'Paul will be in prison by the time he is 18.'

Well, I fucking wasn't, was I?

Then again, neither was she.

When I learned that Prescott was already due to get out, I was furious. How the fuck could that even be possible? The ironic thing is that, to me, Coral was probably the worst of any of them, because she could get into your head and your thoughts and tell you what a piece of shit you were until you had completely internalised this notion and believed it. She was pure evil and I will never understand her motivation. I can only hope that she dies a bitter, lonely death when her time comes.

After the criminal case, a civil case, in the form of a group action, was taken by all the children who had been damaged in the course of their childhoods at St Leonard's. Before the civil case, all the victims of the St Leonard's case were sent to a posh hotel in the West End of London to be interviewed by a psychologist for the class action against London Borough of Tower Hamlets. Our state of mind had to be assessed in order to determine damages.

When the civil case was settled out of court, the most any of the plaintiffs got for the dreadful childhoods they had endured was £25,000, which went to the families of the kids who had died. Most of them had still been very young, in their late teens and early twenties when they died. That is how much the court decided their lives were worth. I got £18,000 in total for my stolen childhood. You can get more sticking your leg in a door or tripping over a pothole in the bloody street. It is insulting.

After the case hit the newspapers, the residents of the fancy estate that had once been St Leonard's found out that some of the roads they lived on had been named after paedophiles. The residents were not impressed, and Havering Council had to rename all the streets. For them, I would assume that this was the end of the story. For the other former residents of St Leonard's children's home – the ones who were still alive – I can only hope that the case and the small amount of money that was provided offered some closure.

Now that I knew just how bad things had been for the other children in the home – so bad that most of my 'brothers' were already dead – it just did not make any sense to me that the people who had committed the abuses were out going through the motions of normal lives, while their victims lay in their graves. I started to think about what I could do to try to even the score. I thought about it long and hard.

12

THE CLOSE CALL

I had spent a lifetime trying to forget my past. I had spent twenty years trying not to be the scared little runt who had grown up in St Leonard's. I had always insisted on standing up to bullies and fighting my own corner.

Now my past was all back with a vengeance. Far from feeling relieved that Bill Starling was doing some time for his crimes, I couldn't stop thinking about all the things that had gone on in St Leonard's, those I had seen and those I had only learned about recently. I felt guilty and ashamed that I hadn't known everything as a young boy and that I hadn't done enough to stop the abuse from happening. I felt bad because here I was, not just surviving but thriving and doing well while so many of the others had already gone to their graves.

Thankfully, I had started having therapy with a man called Terence Watts not that long before the case. If I hadn't, I wouldn't be writing this book now. I would be dead, too. Dead or in prison. Or, most likely, dead in prison.

Terence Watts really helped me. He asked me questions that were probably textbook stuff, but that I found very useful.

'When you were being abused and you were a child, was it your fault?' he asked.

'Well, I don't know.' I found it difficult to listen to questions like that, but I stuck it out because I knew that I needed help to cope with the emotions that were bombarding me from all sides, threatening to overwhelm me and take over my life completely.

'Well, you are an adult now, aren't you? Go back as an adult to you as a child. What would you want to do with that child?'

'Well, I would want to protect him, wouldn't I? I would want to take care of him. He's just a little kid...'

'Right. So have you been mistaken in blaming yourself for what happened to you and for how you reacted? You didn't do anything wrong, and yet you are blaming yourself.'

'I suppose so.'

Terence helped me a lot with the task of vocalising my feelings. But I couldn't shake off the awful feeling of guilt that I had survived and even made a good life for myself when so many of the others had died, and in such dreadful ways. I felt that I had to find a practical solution to how I was feeling; one that didn't have very much to do with the gentle atmosphere of the therapist's office.

As soon as the air cleared after the case, I made a plan. I paced around my house until it came to me. I had always felt safe there, or at least as safe as I ever did, but now I felt hemmed in, unhappy, desperate and angry. I felt sure that I needed to do something drastic, something serious.

Quickly, the solution to these feelings came to me. I was going to kill Auntie Coral – Bill was in prison and unavailable for the present but with any luck I would be able to deal with him later – Alan Prescott and the others. I was going to kill them all for the sake of the many children whose lives they had destroyed. I was going to wipe them out. I didn't think many people would cry after they had gone. I knew that they deserved to die, and I also knew that I had both the means and the ability to give them what they had coming to them.

That very day, I called up some old acquaintances I hadn't spoken to in quite a while and arranged to get a gun. It didn't take long to organise; it never does, if you know who to call. My weapon was top of the range and I knew how to use it. It was a classic; a Browning, with a clip with ten bullets in the bottom and one shot in the barrel. Brownings are easy to load and eleven shots should have been enough to take out the people I was planning to kill. I had been told by people who know that a Browning would be the best for the job because they are easy to use, reliable and clean. They don't make a mess, and they do the job they are made to do effectively and well. I had no interest in hurting my intended victims or making them suffer. I just wanted them to cease to exist.

Unbelievable as it seems, Alan Prescott was still working for Tower Hamlets so it wasn't that hard to find him. I watched him for about a week. I watched Coral for three full days. It was hard to believe that, all this time, she had been living just a few miles away from me. It was astonishing that our paths had never crossed.

I approached my task with all the profession-alism and sobriety of a big-game hunter. I needed to understand my prey; how they thought, moved, behaved. Where they went and what they did. This was a very important job, and there was no way I was going to let myself fuck it up. They all did the same things over and over again. I developed a plan to assassinate them all in the course of a single day so as to minimise the risk of getting caught before I had time to take them all out. It was very difficult watching them covertly without doing anything. I was so angry that I could have torn them apart with my bare hands and a big part of me wanted to see the horrified shock on their faces when they realised that the man who was killing them was none other than one of the children whose lives they had made so very miserable. In fact, nothing would have given me greater pleasure – but the Browning was more of a sure method and I didn't want to leave any room for doubt or failure.

The funny thing was how very ordinary they all looked after all these years. Auntie Coral was just an elderly lady with wattles and too-bright lipstick on her wrinkled lips. Even Alan Prescott was just a pathetic, small, fat old man. Bill was in jail, but his picture was splashed all over the local newspapers. I had remembered Bill Starling as a big, aggressive man who had dominated any room he walked into, but now he was a pathetic little old creature. The sort of little old man you would pass on the street without giving a second thought to. They all looked weak, frail, vulnerable and devastatingly ordinary and seemed to be shadows of the terrifying creatures who had dominated my childhood. How could these less than ordinary people have obliterated the hope of so many children and led to so many untimely deaths?

I made sure that none of them ever saw me, although I am sure that they wouldn't have recognised me if they had. I imagined their deaths over and over again until I could practically taste the blood spatters when I licked my lips in satisfaction after the bullet went in and they keeled over. I had killed them in my head on countless occasions as a child and now, finally, my dreams were about to come true. I just knew that I had to accomplish my goal in the course of a single day, because, if I was apprehended after killing just one, the rest would go free. The challenge was that Auntie Coral was in Essex while the rest were in London. I decided that I would do Prescott first, then Auntie Coral. Bill would have to wait as he was in prison. If I managed not to get caught, I would have something special in store for him when he finally got out. They would be clean, execution-style killings, just one in the back of the head. They would not suffer, much as they deserved to. It would be easier this way.

I told my therapist what I was planning. His reaction was interesting. He provoked me. He said, 'Well, fine, do it. They deserve it, don't they? But think about what killing them will do to you.'

'I don't fucking care what happens,' I said. 'At least I will have avenged Liam and all the rest of them. At least I will have brought death to people who deserve it. If I manage to take them out, it means that my life is worth something and that I have done something to help make things right.'

'So you want to go to prison at thirty-six and spend the rest of your life there? Because that is what is going to happen if you do go through with this plan.'

'If that's what it takes, yeah. If that is what I have to do, then I will do it.'

Terence advised me to watch a film called *Sleepers*. The story line is very similar to mine: a bunch of guys who had been abused as children kill their abuser and get away with it, but their lives are destroyed because they succumbed to the temptation to commit violence and became as bad as the man who had hurt them in the first place.

Terence's message to me was: 'If you bury them, you are burying yourself as well.' He told me that I could win by not letting Bill Starling, Coral and the other abusers beat me, and by not letting myself succumb to the urge to kill them. I could win by going on to live my life successfully and well and by being the better man that Auntie Coral had always told me I could never be. He said that by being happy and breaking the loop I could avenge the deaths of Liam and the others in a way that no killing could ever do and that that would be the best revenge I could take on Starling and the rest of them.

They will never know how close they came to going down in a blaze of gunfire. I went right up to the verge, and stood there for a long time, looking into the abyss. I had followed them for a week with my gun, ready at any moment to take them out.

Back at the house, I sat and looked at the gun. I felt deflated and ashamed. What if Terence was wrong? What if it would really make much more sense to kill them while I had the chance? For a black moment, I thought that maybe it would be for the best if I died instead of them, and joined the rest of the boys from St Leonard's. I took my Browning and shoved it deep into my mouth until the barrel of the gun tore at the delicate tissue of my palate. I could taste the gun metal mingling with my own blood as I almost gagged. I knew that oblivion could be just a second away and that I wouldn't have to feel anything. All I needed to do was pull the trigger, and then all my self-doubt, blame and recriminations would be gone, gone forever.

But, thankfully, I could still hear the voice of Terence telling me that the only way I could really defeat them was to go on and be the better man they had always told me I couldn't be.

I took the gun out of my mouth and looked at it. The Browning is an elegant piece of machinery, but now it looked dark and hideous in my grasp. My hand was trembling. The gun was dark grey and ugly and with a shudder I realised how close I had come to doing something awful. I drove into London – dangerously, because it was hard to see the road through the tears that fell thick and fast from my eyes – and threw the gun into the silent Thames, because I knew that if I kept it I would use it, on myself if not on them. It splashed once and then sank into the dark water along with my plans to avenge the deaths of the children I had grown up with.

The overwhelming sensation I experienced on throwing the gun away was guilt, and that is a feeling that has never completely left me. Then, I fell to my knees right there on the riverbank. I was crying like a baby. I had felt that, if I killed them, I would be doing something for Liam and the other kids I had walked away from all those years before, without so much as a backward glance. Getting rid of the gun felt like walking away from them all over again.

I didn't know whether I wanted to go on living at all at that point. It had taken enormous effort not to kill myself. I wish that I knew for sure that Liam and the rest of the kids would have approved of the decision. It was a long drive home that evening, and many nights before I could sleep properly.

Despite the many wonderful things that have happened to me since, a huge part of me is still sure that I made a horrid mistake and that I should have killed the bastards while I had the chance. Some of them have paid something for their crimes, but they haven't paid nearly enough and I don't believe in a just God who punishes the wicked after death. I wish that I did because, if anyone ever deserved fire and brimstone, it was them. There are still nights when I wake up, thinking about what I nearly did and regretting that I did not see it through, because they really had it coming.

Bill Starling, Auntie Coral, Alan Prescott and

the others will never pay for all the terrible things that they have done. Not unless someone else finishes the job I started.

I can but hope.

13

MOVING ON AND GROWING UP

B y the time I reached my late thirties, I was sure that love, marriage and the baby in the carriage were never going to happen for me. It wasn't that I hadn't had success in romance. Quite the reverse: plenty of women had come and gone from my life and most of them had been great, attractive, intelligent women who would have made any man proud to have them by his side. There had been a couple of close calls when I had been sure, for a while, that I had found Ms Right. But real, enduring love had not happened for me and by now I felt that it most probably never would. I had managed to stay out of prison and I had a steady and reliable career, but I thought that I was probably too old to meet someone and have a family. I also suspected, privately, that this was probably for the best and that I could never be a good father, as I had never had a role model to follow.

The thought that really terrified me and had perhaps been one of the greatest obstacles to reaching a mental state of readiness for a committed relationship was that I would provide a bad example or, heaven forbid, even be an abusive father to any children that I might have. I knew that I would never hurt a child sexually – never that – but I was scared that I would lash out in anger in a thoughtless moment and then have to live with the knowledge that I had hurt a defenceless child. I feared that I wouldn't be able to break out of the vicious circle that had begun the day my mother left me out with the rubbish. That I would repeat the behaviour that I had seen around me every day of my childhood.

I honestly believed that a normal life was simply not an option for me and I had become reconciled to growing old and ending my days alone. I quite consciously put all thoughts of an eventual committed relationship and children out of my mind and concentrated on my career and on creating a life that I could enjoy as a bachelor.

Then I had a wake-up call.

It was 1999, and millennium night was coming up, so everybody and his mother wanted to go out and whoop up a big party. There was a huge demand for doormen, and a friend of mine asked me to do a night's work.

'Nah,' I said. 'I don't do door work any more. I don't need to and I don't want to.'

'Come on, mate, we're really short and you would be helping me out. It's a thousand quid for the night, too.'

'A thousand? All right then. Just to help you out.'

It was against my better judgement. I was the worst guy to be doing door work, the most volatile there was – I know that now. I did not want to run the risk of getting into trouble. But trouble had a habit of finding me.

That night, two customers started causing trouble in the club. I managed to get them outside on my own, but the two doormen who were supposed to help me walked away and left me on the door on my own by mistake. One of the idiots I was throwing out bit me and took a chunk out of my chest. What a scumbag! I went absolutely ballistic and beat the living daylights out of the pair of morons in the car park, leaving one of them with a broken jaw and both of them in a heap on the floor.

That was the last time I have ever been involved in any violence at all with anyone because it shocked me to the core. I realised that I could no longer put myself in situations that could turn violent, because my own strength and determination to stand up for myself could put me in a lot of hot water. I am a model of restraint now, and I have done no door work ever since, because I can see now that it is just asking for trouble. Even when I am cut off in the car, or given the finger, I just grit my teeth and get on with things. Back then, I realised that, if I wanted my life to be good and meaningful, the only person who could ensure that was me. I had been advised by my therapist that the best way to get revenge on the people who had hurt me was by living a good and happy life and I decided that I would do whatever I could to make that happen.

As a child and adolescent, I had been told more times than I could remember that I was going to go to jail. Well, I had come perilously close, but I hadn't been put behind bars because I hadn't done anything wrong. I had no intention of letting anything of the sort happen now that I was straight as a die, and I was going to stay that way. I was also quite confident that I had plenty to offer the world, if only I could find a way to channel all that I had learned and experienced in my professional life. With more determination than I had ever felt before, I set about growing up and developing a career that would stand me in good stead in the future.

I was already working with some of the rapidly growing fitness chains, and I felt that this environment offered me ample scope in which to develop for now, so I started to learn more about the corporate ladder and how I might be able to fit in. With application and a lot of elbow grease, I started to move into progressively larger gyms until I was in a senior position at one of David Lloyd's newly opened mega-clubs. While I worked as a senior personal trainer myself, I also found out that I loved to teach and that I was good at it and soon I was finding, training and mentoring new personal trainers, some of whom were twenty years younger than me. I had – and still have – a real passion for my profession, because I have seen for myself, time and time again, how it makes a real, lasting difference in people's lives. I liked to see the eagerness in the eyes of the new generation of trainers that was now coming to me for advice. I was nearly forty and, as far as some of these young guys were concerned, I was a senior citizen!

It was great to see that the new generation of personal trainers were approaching their careers with focus. I built a team of young professional trainers and taught them everything I knew, not just about the physical exercises they would have to teach, but about how to manage and motivate clients and how to show them that the hard work they do today will pay positive dividends in the future. I honestly believe that physical wellness is a key ingredient to a happy life and it felt good to know that I was enabling these young trainers to reach a position whereby they would be able to go out into the world and make a tangible, meaningful difference in people's lives. While it took some time for me and the administrators of the club to see eye-to-eye on the details of what we were doing, they were happy with the money coming into the club from the growing personal-training business, and I was learning a great deal about how a business is run. This continued and grew in the South East region and then across the country until a team of 'professional consultants' came to head office and decided that, using their PowerPoint and Excel skills, they could do better...

Between one thing and another, it was time for me to set up on my own. I left the David Lloyd club, ignored other invitations to work with the big companies and went into business on my own, working with clients in their own homes and at their own pace and developing a network of trainers in Essex providing similar services. I had realised, in working as a mentor to other personal trainers, that my greatest strengths came not when I focused on myself and what I needed to do, but rather on how to help others, be they other professionals or clients. I had never known, until then, that I was good at communicating and explaining things in a way that most people seemed to like and understand. By now, I had learned that to offer the best service as a personal trainer what you need is commitment, patience and an awareness of what clients need, rather than the baggage that inevitably comes with the corporate environment.

By working in people's homes, I was able to offer them privacy, security and the knowledge that they could discuss their needs with me without having to worry about what others thought. Busy parents, older men and women and those with specific physical problems all found it easier to exercise and train in the comfort of their own homes, far away from unflattering mirrors and the judgemental eyes of other gym-goers.

Seeing how my workouts and expertise helped these people to improve the quality of their lives and their health made me feel very good about myself and confident that the many years that I had spent studying – really ever since that very first day in Dagenham Boxing Club – were paying dividends, both emotionally and financially. As I became better known in the area, I started to get more and more coverage in the local newspapers, providing them with copy and material and sometimes writing columns for them. I was getting good at working with the media. As well as featuring frequently in the print media, I was invited to take a regular health and fitness slot on the local BBC radio channel, BBC Essex, and grew comfortable talking live on radio and handling phone-ins. As the Internet grew in importance, I started to use it more and more to publicise what I could offer, extend my knowledge and share what I was up to with others. I attended training courses and studied as hard as I could to ensure that I remained on top of my profession.

By now an established member of the fitness and health community in the South East, I continued training, mentoring and encouraging others into the industry, and developing those who wanted to progress further. I am really proud that some of my former protégés now have their own studios or gyms and are all good friends.

My past occasionally reared its ugly head. When I was nominated as a candidate for the local businessman of the year awards by a journalist in my area, my first reaction was not pride, but terror. The other men and women up for the award were all 'toffs', I thought, and not the sort of people who would want to sit at a black-tie function with someone like me. I felt quite sure that they would laugh at me when I turned up for the ceremony in my suit and dickey bow and borrowed shiny black shoes! I thought that they would make fun of me. Of course, nothing of the sort happened, because I am not the little scruff I used to be; I have actually become a respectable member of the local business community. This realisation was one of the most surprising that I had ever had, and I was even more astonished to realise that not only did other people respect me, but also that I was beginning to respect myself. For years, I'd had to pinch myself every time something good happened to me. Now, I was beginning to be able to accept my adventures as something I had actually earned.

And there were many adventures. I had long enjoyed watching American Football. Who would have thought that I would enjoy a private box at Candlestick Park in San Francisco courtesy of Silicon Valley billionaire Ray Lane, or attend Calvin Klein's party on Shelter Island with the owner of a New York-based model agency and some of her clients? How could that little boy, working so hard in the boxing ring, have grown into this tall, confident man teaching master classes at Le Sport in St Lucia and sharing drinks with an old icon of mine, the 'Green Goddess' Diana Moran, in the small Caribbean airport (and getting her just a little tipsy)?

There were still times when I was sure that I didn't belong with all these nice, upper-class toffs and even moments of sheer panic when I thought, I can't go in there! That's not for me; they'll make fun of me. Ian tells the story of when we were first at Le Sport and how convinced I was that I wouldn't fit in with 'those sort of people' – only for him to come down to breakfast the next morning and see that I was already on first-name terms with everyone. I told myself and gradually came to understand that it didn't matter any more where I had come from and who I had once been. All that mattered now was that I was someone who had worked hard to become a respected professional and that it was perfectly fine for people to like me for myself, because there was no longer any reason for anyone to cross the street when they saw me. I had changed, too. I was no longer attracted to the dark side. I no longer needed to prove myself with my fists and my ability to survive any attack. Although I will always have to go on proving myself, by this stage I knew that there were other, better ways than that.

Yes, life was good. Best of all, I knew that I had worked long and hard for all the good things that I was enjoying and that I deserved them. Although I was nearly forty, I had only just finished growing up – I had done more maturing in the previous four or five years than in the twenty before – and become the adult man that my unresolved past had never allowed me to be before.

Finally, I could see that I did deserve to be happy.

But did I deserve to have someone special in my life, someone who would stay with me always? Well, perhaps... but I hadn't found her yet.

14

MY HAPPY
ENDING

Then I met Jo, a beautiful woman fourteen years younger myself. It was about four years after I had been cleared of GBH and GBH with Intent and I was still living in Essex and working as a senior personal trainer. Jo was one of the clients at a club where I was working at the time. One day, I was putting a client through her paces, having left some equipment in front of a mirror with the intention of picking it up later. Assuming that the barbell was for anyone to use, Jo picked it up and I went over to set her straight. That was our first encounter. We didn't exchange too many words but I was struck by how pretty she was.

A few weeks later, Jo was training again. I offered her a free training session and got her mobile number. Cunning, eh? Just as we were talking, my mate Ian rang.

'I can't talk to you now,' I whispered into the

phone. 'I've just got chatting with a really hot bird.'

But I was already beginning to realise that Jo wasn't just a hot bird. Shortly after our first date, I invited her to a party. The next day, I took her out again, and after that we started seeing each other every day. I had been seeing two other girls, but I realised that Jo was special and devoted myself exclusively to her. I realised that I could – finally – concentrate on a real, adult relationship based on mutual love and respect. That was eight years ago and, although I didn't realise it then, it was the beginning of a new life for me. Even after Jo and I started going out, I still thought that I was too old to settle down and become a family man. Fortunately, Jo helped me to see otherwise – plus, she was fourteen years younger than me and obviously keen to have kids herself. I realised that what I felt for Jo was more than enough to make me want to settle down and stop my bachelor ways. Suddenly, it was time to grow up and become what I had never expected: a respectable, middle-class man in a tidy suburb with a pretty partner and two wonderful children.

Where I live today isn't very far, in geographical terms, from the hell where I grew up. But it couldn't be further away in terms of environment and atmosphere. Ironically, the money that I got from the Mapperton case gave Jo and me the deposit we needed to buy our family home. Over the years, I had imagined various destinies that seemed possible. I had imagined being a professional boxer. There was a time when I could have seen myself going into security full-time. In my darker moments I had feared that Starling and Coral might have been right about me, and had imagined a life behind bars. This life that I have now, in a comfortable family home with carefully groomed lawns and neighbours who wave hello in the morning, is one that I never envisioned – not in a million years.

Jo is the perfect person for me. She is deeply moral. She is from a nice family, she doesn't like swearing and she really believes in right and wrong in a very straightforward way that is both refreshing and reassuring. Jo has taught me how to behave myself. I was thirty-nine when I met her, and I was sure that I was never going to settle down now, that it was too late for me. Jo showed me that I still had time. On only one occasion has Jo seen the darkness inside me. We were in our car when another driver made me angry. I started yelling and dragged him out of the window of his car. I didn't hurt him; I just scared him a little bit and then got back into the car with Jo and drove off. Poor Jo was so scared and shocked by what I had done that she started to hyperventilate, and I felt so awful about having upset her that I resolved then and there never to do anything of the sort again. And

I never have. Until that moment, reacting with sudden, ferocious anger whenever anyone pissed me off seemed to me to be perfectly normal, rational behaviour. Jo has helped me to see that this behaviour is not rational, and that it is not normal. She keeps me in line. She says, 'Who cares if he is being rude to you from his car? He isn't hurting you. Ignore him. Why are you getting so angry?' And, because I care about what she thinks of me, I listen to her. Thanks to her, I have learned to be able to get angry without acting on that anger.

Nonetheless, I don't feel guilty about many of the road-rage and other small incidents I have been involved in over the years. Most of them deserved it. The ones I hurt were big, capable men who were being aggressive and they were looking for trouble. Even at my most violent, I have always retained a sense of right and wrong. I haven't hurt women, or people who are clearly smaller and weaker than me. I would never hurt a man with children in his car.

About two years after Jo and I got together, our eldest son Harley was born. I remember the moment of his birth. I remember his first smile as if it was yesterday; I will always remember that. Now we have another son, Archie, just as lovely as his older brother.

Harley's birth was the most important moment in my life because it was the start of a whole new chapter and a series of fantastic beginnings. Not only did I have a wonderful new son, but I had been given the opportunity to live my childhood all over again. But this time I would be living it through my own children, and I would be in a position to ensure that nothing bad would ever happen to destroy what is supposed to be the very best part of someone's life. When Harley took his first breath, I went in an instant from being a man who had always felt that he had nothing to lose, to a new, vulnerable creature I did not recognise: the man who has everything to lose. This feeling of vulnerability, and the knowledge that I have the power to give my children the lives they deserve, or screw their lives up, was almost as overwhelming as the waves of love that I felt for my newborn son. I had never thought that I was capable of such deep, all-encompassing love. Now, as I see my kids listen to and absorb every word I say, I often feel overwhelmed by the whole thing. At last, in my mid-forties, I have had to find a new way of being a man, and not the frightened little child that I have been for most of my life. Most of the time, I am not that child, but I know that he will never completely leave me, and that I will take him to my grave with me.

Since I became a father, I have become a different person. There are days when I look in the mirror and fail to recognise the man looking back at me. Who is that guy with the gentle expression and the remains of the baby's breakfast drying on his shoulder? Surely that can't be me!

New parents are always inundated with advice, and most of it is easy to forget, but I received one piece of advice that I will always remember. It came from a friend of mine, who had been a fellow doorman with me years earlier. He came to visit baby Harley when he was just a little scrap and after he had admired him he took me aside and said, 'Look in the mirror, because if you don't like what you see you need to change it because your kids will become you. If you have a road-rage incident, your kid will grow up to experience road rage; if you scream and shout, your kid will scream and shout. You want to look in the mirror and stop the behaviour you don't want your kid to emulate.'

As my children get older, I am more and more aware of how much they learn by imitating their parents, and how much they idolise them. It is daunting, but it also makes me determined to do and be the very best that I can all the time so that, when my children imitate me, they are imitating the sort of person I want them to grow up to be. I certainly don't want either of them to be anything like the man I used to be.

Since my children were born, I don't hate any more, or at least I don't hate like I used to. It isn't in me, although I sometimes feel it in a slightly absent way as amputees are said to feel a missing limb. The only way I can explain it is by saying that I used to blame my life on everybody else, and didn't take responsibility for my own actions. When Harley was born, I realised that I had to be responsible for my own actions and that life wasn't all bad; not now that I was the father of this wonderful child and the partner of this wonderful woman. Best of all, I am not a bad father. I am not the bad example that I feared I would be and I have never once even come close to lashing out in anger. I am a good father who takes care of his children and I see their love for me in their eyes as they must see mine for them. Now, if someone is aggressive to me when I am driving, I ignore them. I ignore them when the children are in the car, and I even ignore them when they are not. Ten years after that eventful flight to Florida, I went over with Harley and Jo, but this time I was the father in one of the nice families on the plane, on my way to Disneyworld. And nothing went wrong.

When my children were born, I also lost whatever feelings I had for my parents. They had always been strangers to me, but they had also been spectres whose absence haunted my life. For a long time, I had harboured deep feelings of great bitterness for my mother, for having abandoned me and for having refused to let me be adopted by anyone else. Now, I feel nothing for her at all. Nothing. As a parent, I can't understand how my mother and father were able to give me and the rest of their children up. I would never let anyone take my babies. I know for myself how deep and strong and primitive the instincts of a parent are, and should be. My mother is still alive. The last time I spoke to her was over thirty years ago, and at that time she blamed everyone but herself for the fact that our family had been broken and destroyed. She is lying, of course. I could be angry but I can't even feel that any more, and I have no intention of ever trying to establish contact. When she left me out with the rubbish, she stole my sense of identity and self-worth and it has taken me the rest of my life to get them back.

However, after becoming a parent, I finally decided to address the issue of my own identity and sense of self, much more for my children's sake than for my own, because I do not want them to grow up without roots and lost the way I did. After years of not wanting anything to do with matters related to my biological family, I finally decided to go to Ireland and see the home of our ancestors in Kilkieran, Connemara. My father had died on 23 April 2005 and his dying wish had been to be buried in his home village. Those children of his who had retained some contact with him had honoured his wishes.

I had not seen my father for thirty years and I had not gone to his funeral. Why go to the funeral of someone you don't know? I didn't feel that I had

anything or anyone to mourn. Now, I left Jo and
Harley at home, flew to Ireland and made my way
to Connemara and the local graveyard to say
goodbye in my own way, if not to my father himself
then to the father I had never had.

At first, I couldn't find my father's grave in the
small cemetery because there were so many
Connollys buried there. Eventually, I found it. I was
completely taken aback by my reaction to the small,
tidy grave. I had expected to feel nothing. Instead, I
just fell to my knees and cried as I had not cried for
years; big racking sobs that made my body shake all
over. I cried like a baby, snot dripping from my nose
and mingling with the thick, hot tears that poured
from my eyes. I didn't understand why I was crying,
because my father had always been a stranger to
me. Looking back now, perhaps the fact that he was
a stranger was the source of my tears. I couldn't
stop. I cried for what seemed like hours. There had
been a caretaker pottering about cleaning up the
cemetery, and he made a discreet exit so as to give
me some privacy.

'I'll come back later,' he said as he passed me. I
couldn't say anything.

When I had cried my tears dry, I left.

Kilkieran is still full of family, and they
welcomed me into their homes as if they had
known me all their lives. It was extraordinary
being with warm, welcoming people to whom I

bore a strong physical resemblance, knowing that, if circumstances had been different, they could always have been part of my life. If my parents had never left Connemara, I might still be there, living in a similar bungalow, working in a local factory or shop. Few if any of my relatives seemed to know much about my family. But they all knew that I was the seventh son of a seventh son, and the old traditions are still very much alive in Connemara. Every time I went to a house afterwards, everyone wanted to hug me and shake my hand and they treated me as though I was lucky and charmed. They also truly believed that I had been blessed with the power of healing, and that I could cure whatever was wrong with them just by touching them with my hands.

I went to look at the family home into which most of my siblings had been born. It was in a modest but pleasant council estate dominated by a huge statue of the Blessed Virgin Mary. Two middle-aged men were sitting outside the house next door and I asked them if they had known the Connollys.

'Oh, for sure I remember the Connollys,' one of them said. 'I used to play with Matthew. He was about my best mate when we were four or five, and then the whole family moved to London.'

If my parents had never left for London, we would all have grown up in Ireland. But it is never too late to work on a relationship, and I am determined that my little boys will know about their heritage and their extended family in Connemara.

Back home, when the children are out with Jo, I sometimes go and stand in their bedrooms. Ours is an ordinary, middle-class suburban home in Essex. To a lot of people, it would probably look like quite a run-of-the-mill house. But to me, it is a palace and the most beautiful place I know. Our children's rooms are clean and nicely furnished and filled with toys. Their windows look out on to green lawns and orderly houses filled with decent, respectable, ordinary families who care for their kids and do their best for them.

Sometimes I try to tell Harley how lucky he is, how good his life is and how wonderful it is that he has nothing to worry about. He can't even begin to understand what I am trying to tell him, because to him a life without fear or hunger or anxiety is natural and normal and right. Being able to provide an ordinary, safe childhood to my sons is the one thing that I am the most proud of.

I look at Harley, my first born. He is tall and strong, intelligent and sensitive. He can already read better than I can, and he exudes confidence. I see him with his mother, Jo, and watch how patient, gentle and kind she is with him. It makes me wonder how I would have been if I had been properly fed and clothed and, more importantly, cared for and loved by a parent who wanted me. One of the proudest moments in my life was when Harley, aged five, was voted 'class councillor' by his teacher and classmates. As he and Archie grow up, they will be able to become whatever they want to be, because they will know that they are loved, and that they have always been wanted. I will never understand why my parents allowed themselves to bring into the world eight children they did not want and did not love.

Thankfully, my children have helped me to become the better man I always wished I was. Much as I do for them, they have done so much more for me. Everything I give them is returned to me in spades.

Providing a safe, stable home for my children also means keeping my psychological issues in check every day. I know that I still have a real obsessive-compulsive disorder, and that I probably always will. I'm well aware of it, so I control it. This is one of my legacies from growing up in care. Because I never feel that I am capable of doing things properly, I check and check again. My house is very tidy, orderly and neat, and I cannot abide it if it gets messed up. The doors all have to be locked and all the lights that should be turned off are turned off. When I am stressed, my OCD reaches unhealthy levels, but most of the time I manage to keep it in check. Personally, I would see my OCD as my safety valve. Because I always want everything to be in control to an extreme degree, I have never been attracted to alcohol or drugs in the slightest. They just aren't my thing.

Today, I am a very happy man and I know that I have a lot to be grateful for. But I am very aware of the fear and rage that are just beneath my surface all the time. I will never be able to sit with my back to the door. I will always have to work very hard to manage not to lash out when someone disrespects me or gets in my way. When I come home in the evening, I lock the doors and then check and check again that they are still locked. I get up at night to check another time. I know that these are things that I will always have to do.

Like most parents, I have realised that my life is not about me any more. It isn't even about whether I like myself or not. Deep down, I still don't like who I am, because I know the depths that I am capable of and I know how vicious and relentless I can be. There is still bad in me. But that is no longer of any consequence. I have even reached the stage where I can see that blame is no longer helpful. At this stage in my life, does it really matter whose fault the whole sorry mess is? I could blame my mother for abandoning me at two weeks old or the state for not vetting people and allowing child abusers and paedophiles to bring us up. But it doesn't make any difference any more. I just hope that today's rejects are being treated better. Some of the clients I work with are social workers. I have asked them if abuse still goes on and if children are better protected, and they assure me that things are not as bad as they once were. I really hope that is true. But I know from my own experience that if children have no sense of identity and no sense of self-worth then any attempts to protect them amount to pissing into the wind.

What I want for my children is for them to be in a position to choose what to do with their own lives. They are bright and they are going to be educated. They will never be attracted to door work or security jobs or the dark side of the street because they will have a thousand other, more attractive options. I am not going to try to live through them, but I am determined for them to have the tools they need to have wonderful, fulfilling lives. I also know that I have to be a good example; that there can be no effing and blinding when someone aggravates me while I am driving or walking around town. I know better than most that children are influenced in every way possible by the things that they see going on around them. I want Harley and Archie to be influenced for the best.

As I have grown older, I have realised that I am not the person I thought I was. I did what I had to do to survive, but, far from being tough and vicious, I am actually quite a sensitive bloke. Don't get me wrong though. If anyone tries to hurt me or mine, I wouldn't think twice...

But, whenever I start to doubt myself or think that life is shit, all I have to do is look into my children's beautiful, open, trusting eyes. Then I tell myself, 'My life isn't that bad. My life is great! I'm not jinxed. I'm not cursed. I don't need to hate.'

And – against all odds – I have proven 'Auntie Coral' wrong.